MW00529559

Nerd Traveler

By
Margaret Montet

Published by

Read
Furiously

Read Often. Read Well.

Copyright 2021 by Margaret Montet

All rights reserved.

Published by Read Furiously. First Edition.

ISBN: 978-1-7371758-1-0

Essay Collection
Non-Fiction
Memoir
Travel

In accordance with the U.S. Copyright Act of 1979, the scanning, uploading, and electronic sharing of any part of this book without the permission of the publisher or creator is forbidden.

For more information on *Nerd Traveler* or Read Furiously, please visit readfuriously.com. For inquiries, please contact samantha@readfuriously.com.

A version of *The Music of Fairies* was previously published in *Furious Lit volume 1: Tell me a Story* by Read Furiously.

A version of *Defending the Waltz King* was previously featured in *Clever Magazine*.

Edited by Samantha Atzeni
Cover Photography by Kira Aud Der Heide

Read (v): The act of interpreting and understanding the written word.

Furiously (adv): To engage in an activity with passion and excitement.

**Read Often. Read Well.
Read Furiously!**

Nerd Traveler is dedicated to my beloved late sister, Audrey Hanlon. She was a tireless and adventurous travel companion, avid reader and book collector, fearless roller coaster aficionado, and Walden Pond circumnavigator.

"The world is a book and those who do not travel read only one page."

--St. Augustine

Table of Contents

Nerd Traveler

When I hit age fifty, I thought: is this all there is? It sounds depressing, but I wasn't depressed. I have a fulfilling librarian job which enables me to be independent and creative, and allows me to champion books and reading. They pay me to be a book nerd. I have good friends and family. I don't have the children and grandchildren that other women my age and older dote on, but I could never imagine myself a mom to little humans. I suspect that little humans I've known can't imagine me as a mom either, but grown men say I remind them of their moms. I get that ALL the time.

I wondered: is the style and situation of life that I have now what I'll have from now on? *Is this all there is?* Is it enough or do I want more, and what would that be? As I focused on writing about places, I found myself learning about people in history. I found that Johann Strauss (the "Waltz King") is so much more than a hack who wrote catchy waltz ditties. I did my best to see Prague with its maze-like streets through Kafka's eyes. I recognized a kindred spirit in Henry David Thoreau who wrote at Walden Pond that he wanted "to live deep and suck out all the marrow of life." I want to suck the marrow out of life, too, but quietly and metaphorically.

I was yearning to write deeper, more literary essays like the kind my literary heroes write (think Paul Theroux, Susan Orlean, Annie Dillard, and John McPhee.) I found a Master of Fine Arts writing program that required attendance at a two-week European residency every summer for three years. (Go big or go home, right?) I hungered for travel and to write about the locations I see through an age-appropriate lens, creating the lyricism of transcendent travel narratives.

I take a lot of notes in small notebooks I can conceal in my handbag. By hiding my little notebooks, I believe I'm concealing my writing nerd tendencies, but I am discovered as soon as I pull out the notebook to record something marvelous. I get some strange looks from people, but I do it anyway. I imagine myself an anthropologist taking important field notes or a detective like Olivia Benson or Harriet the Spy. (Wait, does Benson ever write stuff down?) I also betray my nerd status when I choose a quiet evening of journaling over dazzling (as I imagine it) nightlife. These hand-written journals are the basis of my essays because in them I have recorded my impressions while they are still fresh. I have a talent for encountering misadventures and being seated near colorful characters in restaurants. The memories that are resplendent enough to remain with me upon my re-entry into ordinary life color my stories with my unique perspective. That's my method, usually.

Please keep this next revelation under your hat. It

may border on the ridiculous. I actually write a short "research proposal" for myself before I embark upon a journey. I might abandon or refine this proposal once I set out to write about the travel experience and how it has changed me, but it helps me focus my attention. (I wouldn't enter a fabric store without a list to stick to or else I'll walk out in debt and with enough 100% cotton fabric for 67 quilts.) My little research proposal helped me in Vienna, for example, where I had limited time and many landmarks from music history to explore. I visited Mozart's house, Johann Strauss's house, the composer statues in the *Stadtpark*, and the Vienna Opera, but Beethoven's and Schubert's houses would have to wait until next time. My research proposal focused me on how Vienna presents its musical heritage. Besides my research proposal, I spend a lot of time preparing for a trip selecting books to read. I need one to read on the plane and an extra for the trip back just in case. Nonfiction with information and history about my destination is great, but I need also light fiction for when there are distractions. I think by now readers will have perceived that my travel curiosity transcend the average and shoots off on a nerd trajectory.

My perceptions of a place, or appreciation of music, art, or literature, are influenced by conversations I have enjoyed with close friends. Stop by my office and tell me what you heard on National Public Radio which reminded you of me. Suggest a walk in nature and we'll talk about a film you've just seen. Accompany me on a day trip to somewhere close which, for some reason, we have not yet visited. Commit to a stress-free weekend jaunt to visit historic homes we've always wanted to see. I'm grateful to have these curious, intelligent people in my life to stretch my mind. Emerson said: "Strict conversation with a friend is the magazine out of which all good writing is drawn." Likewise, I treasure visits with friends and family in my original hometown of Cape May, not simply for the companionship, but because they, without fail, show me new ways to appreciate this familiar place so close to my heart.

I noticed this: Mom and Dad kept showing up in my writing. They are where I'm from. I'm from Cape May, too, and Hamilton, New Jersey, and Philadelphia. I'm from family, friends, teachers and chance encounters. My parents have both been gone for years, but the fact that they and their values still influence my existence reminds me how much I miss them. A trip to the beach makes me think of Dad trying to teach me about shore birds. A movie-locations tour in Manhattan reminds me of my attempts to break through my Brooklynite mom's dementia with movies she might recognize. They were both old enough to be my grandparents, actually, and their wisdom and experience (though I didn't always appreciate this when I was a teenager) made me into the quiet, temperate, cautious adult (okay, nerd) I've always been. Dad was a fatherless eight-year-old Cajun lad in Louisiana when his widowed mother packed him and his six siblings up for a Great Migration north to Chicago. The opportunities they found were limited, and soon they'd battle the Great Depression. During World War II he met my mother on an ice-skating rink in Brooklyn, and they married in 1943.

In 1950, they bought this house in Cape May where I sit right now. Thirteen years after that, I appeared on the scene and changed everything, especially their visions of quiet retirement at the seashore. They were settled, experienced, wise, and somewhat out-of-date, and that's where I came from.

What would a travel essay about me look like? It would look dull unless the reader had the ability to get inside my head and see what I marvel at, and how I put what I learn into the context of what I see. Along with the desire to write deeper, more significant travel pieces, I yearn to write about (what I gather is) the peculiar way I enjoy travel. I like to learn about the history, culture, and nature of a place through books and lectures, I enjoy attending concerts and performances, I eat popular native cuisine within reason (*Weiner Schnitzel* squirted with lemon and *churros con chocolate*, I adore you), and I challenge myself with unfamiliar languages (*Zut alors!*). Some of this reinforces my claims of nerd status. I decided to write about my adventures and travels from my position of quiet nerdiness in the hopes of bringing understanding and compassion for people like me (nerds) to the world.

Writing is discovery, I've read, and this brings me to another thread that winds through my stories: age. It's not the same to travel as a fifty-year-old as it was as a thirty-year-old. There are prescription refills to plan out, and fatigue to consider, but at the same time the occasional discounts if you carry that red card. Although I don't dwell on my accumulation of years, I'm reminded of them when I watch younger travel companions with boundless energy, or find myself looking forward to quiet pajama'd journaling time in the evening. Way back in a 1625 essay, Francis Bacon said this: "Travel, in the younger sort, is part of education; in the elder, a part of experience." Travel is both for me, honestly. My travel writing heroes share musings on aging, too. Once I thought these observations tedious, but now I identify. There was the time in Hollywood when I was struggling to remember Angela Lansbury's name because I saw the drugstore where she was discovered, and I'll need to mention that in my story. All I could come up with was "Jessica Fletcher," the name of the senior-citizen mystery-writer she portrayed on TV. It was a *bona fide* senior moment. There was a time I made fun of people who watched that show, and now it is one of my favorites. I know the actress's name—why could I not remember it?

We'll start and end in Cape May, my original hometown at the southern tip of New Jersey, where I've been a part-time resident all my life. After Dad's stint in the U.S. Coast Guard, our little family moved north so he could hold a series of government jobs in order to support this new little bundle of joy. ("This one's going to want to go to college!" I can hear him saying.) I attended school in our more northern residences all the while knowing that my parents would move back to Cape May the first chance they got. I'd live there full-time now if I could, but peninsular Cape May job-seekers are limited to a northerly direction when searching for positions. (That's why I call Cape May my "original" hometown.) The stars have not been aligned for me yet in that regard, but I am grateful that my sister and I are able to share ownership of our parents' home there. It's where I do big chunks of my writing and I can't imagine life without the place. This life of bouncing between idyllic Cape May and a more practical point north for work and school has been a way of life since age four, and has enabled me to see Cape May as a native (I was born here) as well as a visitor. At the same time, I feel something like a foreigner in both places at times.

That sense of being a foreigner is compounded by outlier feelings. I almost said this to a fellow human recently, but stopped myself in the nick of time: "She reminds me of you, in that way you make fun of me for any part of me that might be different from you. She does that, too." This is what I want to say to people who think I'm too quiet, too sober, too fat, not hip enough, not interested in reality television enough, or not athletic enough. I'm different, it's true, and this truth has become apparent to me especially when I travel or when I secretly compare my adventures to others'.

I consider adventures the experience of opera, literature, classical music, old movies, and visual art. These kinds of art challenge me. I was surprised, but not really, to notice that classrooms and books appear in most of my essays: me as a young student, an older student, or a teacher. Classrooms have been very important in my life, whether that classroom is traditional, a band practice room, a graduate seminar room, the Game Room at the retirement village where I teach, or a hotel conference room. They show up in my dreams, too, and books often line the walls of my dream scenes. This, I believe, is unquestionably nerdy.

I like to be told stories and I like to tell stories. In *Nerd Traveler*, we'll start in Cape May, and then travel to New York City, Pittsburgh, Washington, DC, Los Angeles, and Concord. Abroad, we'll explore Prague, Vienna, Dublin, and Galway, and excursions from these cities. There won't be any drinking or debauchery in mine, no opium dens or camel rides across a desert, but there will be culture and whimsy. Music, books, and movies are irresistible to me. They feed my amazement and understanding of a locale. My interest in Franz Kafka's stories was nearly undetectable until I went to Prague. My connection to Ireland was almost imperceptible until I went there and listened to folk tales and music while learning about the geography. I'm hoping my stories of place will delight you, transport you, and shift your perspectives on these places. If they do, even just a little bit, my Nerd Traveler sobriquet will have even more value.

Sherlock and Mycroft Visit Cape May

During Cape May's Sherlock Holmes Weekend, participants comb the Victorian city and some of its iconic homes for clues to a complex mystery.

"Come, Watson, come! The game is afoot."

Sir Arthur Conan Doyle,
The Return of Sherlock Holmes (1904),
"The Adventure of the Abbey Grange"

Sherlock Holmes was young and handsome and his father was seated at my table. Dr. John Watson was even younger and Mycroft Holmes had a distinctive twenty-first-century look. The actress portraying Lady Abigail, the Actress, came back after that character's death to portray Inspector Lestrade of Scotland Yard. As we ate our chocolate mousse with whipped cream and rainbow sprinkles, these thespians acted out the first installment of an original Sherlock Holmesian mystery at the Inn of Cape May. The play's audience was now a gang of deputy detectives charged with solving the mystery. After this Friday night performance, we'd receive our detective worksheets and learn which five historic locations in Victorian Cape May, New Jersey, we would scrutinize in Saturday afternoon's Search for Clues Tour. This city is known as America's First Seaside Resort, and the locations of the mystery play and clues were close enough to the Atlantic Ocean to hear the breakers crashing on shore, smell the salt air, and feel the sea breezes. I had a plan to buy some chocolate-dipped pretzel rods (I like to eat them as I drive home on Sunday nights) and salt water taffy at the candy store during Saturday's amateur gumshoe work.

March in Cape May is for Sherlock Holmes and for preparing for the summer beach season. In most New

Jersey shore towns, the "season" officially starts on Memorial Day Weekend. In Cape May, the "season" starts in April with the Spring Festival. Gardens are already cleaned up in March and feature early crocuses, hyacinths, tulips, and flowering shrubs and trees. After the cold and quiet months of January and February shops and restaurants start to come alive because of Sherlock Weekend, the Singer/Songwriter Festival, and birders with binoculars looking for migrating birds and resident shorebirds. Road construction occurs now that winter is over, and this year Myrtle and Hughes Avenues were excavated for infrastructure replacement. Because of the rain, they were a muddy mess for Sherlock Weekend.

The City of Cape May is an especially good match for Sherlock Holmes mysteries mostly because of an 1878 fire. It destroyed much of the central part of the town, and when homes, inns, and other businesses were rebuilt, they were constructed in the contemporary Victorian style. The original Sherlock Holmes would feel right at home in Cape May because creator Arthur Conan Doyle set his mysteries during this era in England. Many of Cape May's Victorian buildings survived and around the time of the U.S. Bicentennial celebration were treated to restorations. Since then, Cape May has meticulously preserved that Victorian personality. New buildings here must be in Victorian style, and paint color choices for any buildings have to be approved by the city. When we were purchasing replacement windows for our house in neighboring Lower Township, the Home Depot salesman checked to make sure we weren't buying these for a Cape May Victorian because vinyl is not allowed. "No," I said, "we're in North Cape May, north of the canal. We can use vinyl." A stroll through the crayon-colored, authentic Victorian city is a delight and prompts historically-inspired daydreams.

This was the third time I participated in the Sherlock Holmes Weekend organized by the Mid-Atlantic Center for the Arts and Humanities (MAC). There's a new play each year, debuted in March and reprised in November. Amateur sleuths flock to this event twice a year. Just like at Bruce Springsteen concerts, attendees have "numbers:" "I've done this 24 times, but she's done it 27!" I'm a "'three" and one couple at my table was a "four." I remember my first Sherlock Weekend: I was nervous because I hadn't read many Holmes mysteries or watched him much in movies or television shows. I was worried that other participants would be Sherlock experts and put me to shame, but my concerns were for naught. Everyone was chatty and friendly and the organizers were welcoming. I enjoyed it, and became hooked on the mysterious detective's adventures.

In the past, I've challenged myself to do all or part of the weekend in costume. I sewed most of my interchangeable costume parts in shades of brown, but I've enhanced my Victorian trousseau with a purchased white blouse and a brown hat with a prominent feather. This is an opportunity to wear those costume jewelry cameo brooches I've acquired over the years, all of them seemingly of the same woman in the same pose. (Spooky.) I've seen some gorgeous costumes here, and both men and women seem to enjoy wearing Victorian style.

This year, the women's gowns were mostly black with red accents and a liberal use of velvet. Men were snappy dressers, too, one with a burgundy-trimmed black velveteen jacket, and another with a black, satin-trimmed top hat. I think I saw a Dr. Watson-style bowler hat on another participant. One year, there was a man dressed as a Victorian woman, and he was among the best-dressed. He did not win a prize, but his gowns were spectacular. That was the year that one young woman expertly sewed both her lavishly embellished gown *and* her escort's suit! I envied her sewing skills.

I have two costume skirts. One is brown cotton twill with a subtle stripe woven into the fabric. This skirt required five or six yards of fabric and it is full and heavy. Paired with my high-heeled Victorian lace-up costume boots, it makes for some difficult walking on Cape May's cracked flagstone sidewalks. One day I decided I needed another skirt for this event and came up with a brilliant idea: my 1992 wedding dress! I sewed that get-up also, simulating a Victorian style by layering white cotton batiste over white cotton lawn. The young saleswoman in a shop on Philadelphia's Fabric Row suggested this to me and I thought it was authentic-looking, especially when I added a flounce in front and trimmed everything with expensive handmade lace. The blouse is too fitted to fit now in my middle-age, but it was a stunner with its row of pearl buttons down the back. All of this was created from a specialty historic sewing pattern, but the hat on my head was improvised: a plain Madeline-style straw hat covered in the same fabrics and lace with some ivory silk roses I found in Cape May.

Well, the marriage didn't work out and the two-piece dress and hat cover sat in a sealed, archival-quality preservation box in the closet in my study. It stayed there until I had the bright idea to remove the skirt, dye it brown, and add it to the Victorian trousseau. After all, what else was I going to use that dress for? The "new" skirt was added to the costume trousseau: two lacey blouses, the heavy full skirt, the hat with a feather, a crocheted shawl, and a bag made out of antique-looking upholstery fabric.

This year I decided to skip the costumes and solve the mystery incognito. Under the radar. In 21st-century street clothes. I like a modest amount of cosplay (the insider term for costume-play), and it certainly adds a layer of escapism to the proceedings. Frankly, though, the costume contests on Friday evening and Saturday afternoon felt creepy. I was standing up with women who bought or rented gorgeous evening gowns and there I was in my humble homespun cottons. People were judging us based on our appearance, and voted on the best ensembles with applause. I was aware of their eyes on my chubby body and dressmaking abilities. A photograph of the contestants one year (including me) landed in the local paper and was charming, but still made me feel uneasy. If the preceding is not enough to justify this year's street clothes decision, consider the icky feeling when a guy at my table asked me if my underthings were authentic. I answered him directly, hoping that he wouldn't be inspired to ask more such questions: "No, I have to admit that, besides my petticoat which is needed to fill out my skirt, my underthings are not Victorian. There's no corset or bloomers on me."

This year my tablemates were not talkative, at least not at first. The couple to my right (she looked something like Katie Couric) was enjoying the weekend as a Christmas present from him to her. They were staying at the posh and popular Queen Victoria Inn, where we were to find one of our clues. The couple to my left was participating for the first time. He looked like Vladimir Putin. The couple across from me let on that they knew one of the actors. The man looked and spoke like Sylvester Stallone. Mrs. Stallone dropped out after the first play installment (Friday evening), he said, because her contact in the thespian group revealed to her the solution to the mystery. A bachelorette party sat at the next table in matching Sherlock-style deerstalker hats, the prospective bride's featuring a cheesy white veil like a sheer curtain covering the back of her neck. The bride-to-be was serious: she took more notes than I did!

I was happy to see that Mycroft Holmes, Sherlock's older brother, had a prominent part in this play. I'm intrigued by this enigmatic character but he doesn't appear in many of Conan Doyle's stories. In fact, for a long time Sherlock's sidekick Dr. Watson assumed that Sherlock was an orphan because he rarely mentioned family at all. When Mycroft is mentioned, he's described as being even better at solving mysteries, or "deducing," than his brother Sherlock, and through his job with the British government has access to government secrets. Sherlock describes him as lazy and pompous and explains that Mycroft's laziness kept him from becoming a high-profile sleuth like Sherlock: "If the art of the detective began and ended in reasoning from an armchair, my brother would be the greatest criminal agent that ever lived. But he has no ambition and no energy." (That's Sherlock describing Mycroft in "The Greek Interpreter.") Mycroft was something of an odd duck—he was a member of the Diogenes Club where there was a rule that members should not acknowledge each other. Sherlock knew he could always find Mycroft at this club at the same time every day and often went there to consult with his brother on cases, unbeknownst to Dr. Watson. This came out in "The Greek Interpreter." Sitting in a Philadelphia Starbucks after the weekend with an associate, I told him about Sherlock Weekend and Mycroft's appearance. He abruptly asked, "Are you a Sherlock or a Mycroft?" It was an unexpected question, and while still processing it I found myself answering slowly, straight from the reptilian brain, "Mycroft." I guess I do identify more with him. (I don't identify as lazy and pompous, however).

Saturday afternoon I parked in my usual meter-free West Cape May parking spot and set out with my detective worksheet. Our Sherlock Holmes Saturday task was this: walk around the city on our own and visit four authentic Victorian inns and one carriage house where we would find clues that may or may not help us solve the mystery. Red herrings abound. I was working alone to solve the mystery this year, since I had been unable to convince anyone that while this may seem nerdy, it is a delightful experience.

So who killed the Actress, Lady Abigail? We amateur detectives visited four Victorian inns in whatever order we wanted. (It's a "self-guided" tour.) I started with the big, green Queen Victoria Inn at the corner of Ocean Street and Columbia Avenue. We are usually limited to the parlors and dining rooms of the inns. I'd been in here searching for Sherlock clues years before and the hosts told us about its stunning custom-replica wallpaper. While I admired the wallpaper, Mrs. Hudson popped in and announced herself. "I'm Sherlock Holmes's landlady." (Is that a clue?) I don't always come up with the best questions for the hosts mostly because my eyes are taking in all the Victorian decoration and artifacts. However, in each inn I had the benefit of running into other participants and hearing the innkeepers' answers to their questions.

I greeted the "Katie Couric" couple from my table in front of the public library on the way to Leith Hall. This bed & breakfast inn is about a block closer to the ocean on Ocean Street, and is tan with a red mansard roof. (Mansard roofs bend over most of the top story of the house and are punctuated by windows. They became popular because in this era taxes were figured by the amount of windows in the structure, but windows popping out from roofs didn't count. With this style roof, homeowners got away with an extra upper floor without paying taxes on it because the windows are surrounded by roof. Now a mansard roof is just a Victorian style choice.)

In Leith Hall I had a hard time figuring out the clue. I was growing frustrated as another visitor voiced the same trouble. The innkeeper, draped casually on the

Victorian sofa advised: "My inn is strictly Victorian, so if you see anything lying around that is not Victorian, regard it with suspicion." But then, "Victorian parlors tend to be cluttered, so it might be difficult to spot the clue." I finally decided that the clue was the set of four tins of stage make-up (or was it paint?) sitting on a table next to a stereoscope with Victorian slides. I wasn't sure how I'd include the make-up in my mystery solution...but wait...do I remember something about make-up containing arsenic? I made my way out the narrow hallway not entirely sure how the make-up tins would figure in to the mystery's solution. Victorians must have been shorter and narrower than us because the walks, doorways, halls and even parlors and dining rooms feel claustrophobic.

The peach and terracotta Henry Sawyer Inn is known for its incredible collection of M.I. Hummel figurines, those cute little German statues of cherubic kids in Lederhosen posing with puppies, kittens, kites, and butterflies. These have nothing to do with Sherlock Holmes but captivated my attention. I almost forgot to look for a clue, but luckily this one was obvious. There was a mismatched teacup and saucer sitting on the sideboard in the dining room. I remembered the Actress character asking for a cup of tea during Friday evening's play. This must have been hers judging from the bold red lipstick on the cup. It signaled to me that I should include her in my mystery solution. As I attempted to leave the Henry Sawyer, I ran into that group of well-dressed Victorian sleuths with the velvet-trimmed gowns and top hats. Other non-costumed amateur detectives asked to take selfies with them, and their photo op on the big, wrap-around porch trapped me inside. No problem—I went back in and gazed at the Hummel figurines. I've heard people don't care much about Hummels anymore, but I like them.

The Bedford Inn is on Stockton Avenue near Howard Street, a few blocks west of the Henry Sawyer. Its façade is unique because of the porch that runs across the full length of the first floor and a matching veranda across the second. Inside, the dining room features a striking but non-Victorian mural depicting contemporary Cape May scenes. The clue here was a paperbound notebook which looked to me to be a script, or maybe performance notes from one of the actors. I couldn't get a good look at it because there was a crowd around it. Either way, the best I could extract from these clues was that the actors that we'd seen so far were involved in the murder. Maybe the next clue would tie it together for me.

The walk from the Bedford Inn to the last clue location was the longest, and by this time it had started to rain, the kind of icy, chilly rain that you feel only by the seashore. Also that Saturday, I felt unsteady on my feet as I walked around historic Cape May enjoying signs of spring and looking for clues to the fictional murder. Something didn't feel right. I wasn't sick, but for some reason I had a sort of premonition that I was going to fall. Those flagstone sidewalks can be slippery in the rain, but I was wearing my sensible brown shoes and had no earthly reason to expect a fall. Why was I feeling vulnerable? Am I getting old? Sick? Have I not had enough sleep?

Maybe I was feeling unsettled because Cape May's Gazebo, much-loved (I thought by everyone) and symbolic, had been demolished. I felt a little queasy looking at Rotary Park without it for the first time. City leaders say it will be replaced by a fine bandstand, and this seems to imply that the quirky summer concerts I have come to love and blog about at the Gazebo (the accordion orchestra, the hobo band, the Philadelphia-style Mummer string band, etc.) will still happen here. Though in order to replace the Gazebo with the bandstand, trees are scheduled to be chopped down. I saw those trees there in the Saturday rain with pink plastic ribbons tied around their trunks marking them for murder.

The park was charming and cozy, right near the Washington Street Pedestrian Mall's shoe store, the proprietor of which, back in the 1960s, called my mother "Size 7." The park makes me think of Mom and me shopping and talking as we walked around Cape May hundreds of times since I was a little girl, all seasons of the year. The city has a year-round population of 3,607 according to the 2010 United States Census, which is actually about 700 persons smaller than when I was a child. Hardy souls live here in the cold weather, too, quietly enjoying the Victorian architecture and the ocean. A few years back, Cape May leaders broke my heart when they decided to tear down the Beach Theater, Cape May's movie palace since 1950. My sister and her girlfriends saw Alfred Hitchcock's *The Birds* there in the early 1960s, eating Sno-Caps and scaring themselves silly for the long walk home in the dark, deserted, off-season shore town. "I never looked at birds the same way again," she told me. I saw *E.T.* there with my high school sweetheart, and more recently watched "Bruce Springsteen in Barcelona." When a group of sophisticated residents banded together in an attempt to save the theater by transforming it into an art film house, I was in heaven. Their valiant attempt failed. I miss that theater, and nothing has been done to "improve" the front portion which survived.

Although the Gazebo was a lovely structure, word is that performers don't like it so much because it is cramped. They can't see their audience gathered in the park because of the fence around the perimeter of the stage that blocks them from seeing us and us from seeing anyone except those standing, usually the conductor and any soloists. Attending these concerts brought me back to my childhood and a less-developed, less-touristy Cape May.

On a December evening at twilight, the City's Christmas tree is there, pretty as a picture with gas-lit streetlights in the background. Perhaps future Christmas trees will be displayed in the swank new bandstand, but I'm hanging on to the past: my photos and memories of that old Gazebo. In 2015, one of my summer Gazebo photographs was used for the city's online listing of summer concerts. That made me feel good—a contribution to Cape May culture.

The fifth Sherlock clue stop was the Carriage House at the Emlen Physick Estate, a restored mansion designed by celebrated architect Frank Furness for Dr. Physick, which is now a Cape May centerpiece. The mansion's adjacent Carriage House is a gift shop and exhibit space with an attached tea room open in the summer. I've only eaten there once, a few years back with a former high school boyfriend passing through town on his Honda Storm motorcycle. All I remember is eating watercress finger sandwiches and having an unprecedented, unexplained, and embarrassing coughing fit. I felt like Typhoid Mary in that lovely tea room, but enjoyed the ambiance once I stopped coughing. This was the one time I ate borscht. The clue we were to examine here was a letter from Lady Abigail informing the play's director that she'd be leaving the show. She didn't say why in the letter, but she seemed to feel compelled to get out of town quickly. What could make her want to leave the show abruptly?

The self-guided Sherlock clue tour took about two hours. The locations were spread out over the city, and I estimate from the condition of my calf muscles afterward that I walked three or four miles. When it started raining a sloppy, partially frozen mix, my deluxe raincoat hood kept my head dry but didn't keep out the chill. After searching for clues, we reported back to the warm Inn of Cape May to watch the next installment of the play and to sip hot tea, eat chocolate chunk cookies, and turn in our first detective sheet. "I'm confident about my theory," I wrote in my detective notebook, "It might be too obvious and simplistic, but I think most of the clues we found at the inns and the lines spoken by the characters led to this explanation."

So how did Sherlock Holmes solve his complex mysteries? Did he have all of that information (history, geography, religion, biography) stored in his brain? He was profiled as an unusually intelligent man, but his creator, Arthur Conan Doyle, supplemented Sherlock's smarts with a device called the commonplace book. Many nineteenth-century readers collected quotes and ideas from their reading and wrote them in their commonplace books which became a curated mishmash of ideas, quotes, diagrams, drawings, maps and other bits. The creator would read through their commonplace book, and with each reading the nascent ideas would spark together, inspire new thoughts, or synthesize with ideas already in the thinker's mind.

These books became popular during the eighteenth-century Enlightenment, a movement in western European and American history when traditions were questioned and new ideas were rational, based on experience and experiment. The United States Declaration of Independence is an example of this mode of thought. Coincidentally, its author, Thomas Jefferson, kept three distinct commonplace books. One of these was the literary commonplace book which he "kept as a young bachelor up until age 30," according to Martha King, a Jefferson scholar at Princeton University Press, which has published two of Jefferson's commonplace books. "There is evidence that he consulted and cited from his literary commonplace book throughout his life. For example, (Jefferson) often quoted lines from Horace or the classics in his correspondence." Commonplace books seemed to be effective also for Jefferson contemporaries Benjamin Franklin, physician and Declaration of Independence signer Benjamin Rush, and the Scottish poet Robert Burns.

And then there's Sherlock Holmes. In "The

Adventure of the Missing Three-Quarter," Sherlock Holmes consults his multi-volume commonplace book to find information about a mysterious man. Dr. Watson writes: "When our visitor was silent Holmes stretched out his hand and took down letter 'S' of his commonplace book. For once he dug in vain into that mine of varied information." Holmes used his commonplace books for research rather than creation.

Before the Cape May mystery solution was revealed at Sunday's lunch, the Courics, the Putins, Mr. Stallone, and I shared our own theories about the murder. Our detective questionnaires were handed in with our creative solutions and trivia answers completed, so it didn't matter if we divulged our secret theories to each other. My solution involved a love triangle between Lady Abigail, the play's director, and one of the young actors. The Putins' solution was close to mine with a few more twists and turns. The Courics had a convoluted theory involving a love child (the same young actor character I had Lady Abigail linked with romantically). This came very close to the actual solution, but not close enough to win them a prize. The grand-prize winner was an uncostumed woman from the other side of the room. She won an envelope filled with cash. (One hundred? Two hundred? I'll let you know someday when I win.) The Clueless Wonder, the participant furthest away from the answer who actually made an attempt, received complimentary tickets for next year's Sherlock mystery. Also at this last meeting over lunch on Sunday someone had guessed that our other tablemate, Mr. Stallone, was related to the actor portraying Sherlock Holmes. "Yes, I am his…father," he revealed with much drama. Mr. Stallone ghosted-out at some point once his son's performance was finished.

I never did fall on the flagstone sidewalks that weekend, but I was glad I hadn't attempted this mystery in high-heeled lace-up boots and long skirts designed to hide my sexy Victorian ankles. I always remind myself that life is a series of phases and perhaps I was going through a phase of vulnerability for some reason. My best guess: they tore down the Beach Theater and now my Gazebo. Cape May is changing! The little city is so much a part of me that I feel its pain.

The weather was unwelcoming but I enjoyed the comforting sensation of hot tea or cocoa and the strolls around my favorite Victorian city. Being here in March gave me a preview of changes to come. I bought my chocolate-dipped pretzel rods for the ride home and some salt water taffy for gifts. No one would figure out all the twists and turns of the mystery story, but the activity was escapist enough to make me forget about life's little stressors. My guy Mycroft was involved in the mystery's solution, but that's all I'm at liberty to say. (I went out on a limb telling you about the clues!) Costumes would have added an extra layer of make-believe to the weekend, but honestly, Cape May's Victorian wonderland does escapism effectively on its own.

Margaret Montet

Transcending Concord

My sister and I followed in Henry David Thoreau's footsteps by circumnavigating his famous muse, Walden Pond.

"Well, that's a dream fulfilled!" My sister, Audrey, was thrilled with Louisa May Alcott's Orchard House. We each read *Little Women* when we were young, saw the three movies, and now finally toured the house where the Alcotts lived. Louisa set her fictional stories in this house and based the characters on herself and her sisters. We saw Beth's melodeon (a small organ), May's art studio, and the half-moon desk their father built in Louisa's bedroom. She wrote *Little Women* on that tiny "half-moon" desk in a matter of months. Imagine that. Orchard House is in Concord, Massachusetts, just down Lexington Street from Ralph Waldo Emerson's house, and a couple of miles from Thoreau's Walden Pond. We toured them, too, and learned that Louisa's father Bronson Alcott, Henry David Thoreau, and Ralph Waldo Emerson were friends and all contributed to Transcendentalism, a philosophical and social movement of the mid-nineteenth century which proposes that divinity is in all nature and humanity.

I wasn't interested in Transcendentalism when I went to Concord. I wanted to finally visit the Alcott house because I'd heard so much about it and fanned those flames by watching the *Little Women* movies. But a strange thing happened: I became interested in Ralph Waldo Emerson and Henry David Thoreau. Emerson is the wise essayist who even as a minister could not reconcile his spiritual beliefs with organized religion. He wasn't anti-social, he claimed in self-defense; he was anti-organizational. "Build, therefore, your own world," he wrote in his masterpiece essay, "Nature." Thoreau, who famously lived in a cabin on the shore of Walden Pond, pursued a "naturalistic individualism." Both men were individualists and self-reliant. Both were misunderstood. I didn't know all this when I arrived in Concord. I was there to look at historic houses. This is what meaningful travel does for us: it shifts our interest in a place whether we want it to or not. My springtime jaunt to Concord to have a look at historic homes turned into a primer on Transcendentalism.

I created this little excursion because I was curious about Louisa May Alcott's house where *Little Women* was set, and because I have an interest in historic homes and how they are presented to the public. I live about ninety minutes away from author Pearl S. Buck's Green Hills Farm in Perkasie, Pennsylvania, and by touring her home I developed a balanced understanding of Buck the author and Buck the person. The information I gleaned there enhanced what I had recently learned from a meticulously researched biography by Peter Conn. The small wooden desk on which she wrote *The Good Earth* is on display there, as well as the honorary doctorates that were bestowed on her, the first Pulitzer Prize for literature won by a woman, keys to various cities, and photographs from her writing career. Buck spent half her life in China (she fell in love with the country because her parents were Southern Presbyterian missionaries), so Chinese artifacts are displayed in the house, too. They are a vital part of Pearl S. Buck's experience. I remember seeing rice pottery, tiny shoes for adult women with bound feet, and beautiful silks. The house tour also focuses on Pearl Buck the humanitarian who set up foundations to help Chinese orphans and mixed-race children no one wanted. She and her husband adopted seven children and I get the impression throughout the property that this was a happy and supportive environment for the family.

On the other hand, I read another meticulously researched biography written by Kristen Iverson about Margaret "Molly" Brown. I got to visit her house in Denver. Unlike the balanced presentation of Buck at her home, the Margaret Brown experience was one-dimensional. We learned only about Brown's Titanic-related adventures. As we toured the home on Pennsylvania Street, we heard about her voyage on the Titanic, its sinking, and a brief mention of her aid to less affluent survivors. Yes, this is the woman known as "The Unsinkable Molly Brown," but she was never actually known as Molly ("Molly" is more singable than "Margaret"), and she was a notable humanitarian before and after the ill-fated Titanic voyage. All of that is lost on the visitor. I came away from that house frustrated and disappointed.

I wanted the Louisa May Alcott experience to be thorough and balanced: more like the Pearl S. Buck tour, and less like the Margaret Brown. But there's more: I wanted to learn more about the Alcotts' neighbors Henry David Thoreau and Ralph Waldo Emerson. Emerson's house is open for tours, and there is a replica of Thoreau's Walden Pond cabin ready to be inspected. I thought I'd scored big with a three-for-one author house pilgrimage, but I would find much more. On a Friday in May, my sister and I drove the six hours or so from New Jersey to Massachusetts in my MINI Cooper, listening to '60's music, and encountering hellacious traffic.

We visited Emerson's house first on Saturday morning, simply because it was the first one we found: from the town center, walk east along Lexington Road and turn right on Cambridge Turnpike. There it is, the big white house on the corner with the white fence around it. Waldo and his wife Lidian moved into the house in 1835, and they raised two daughters there. It's a typical nineteenth century home with four rooms on the first floor and four on the second, and it was later enlarged by the Emersons. The home barely survived a serious fire in 1872. The family's neighbors and friends made arrangements to have the house fixed after the fire, helped pay for the repairs, and sent the family to Europe to distract them. Thoreau used to visit here often, not only to discuss lofty Transcendental thoughts with Waldo, but to entertain the Emerson children. My favorite items in the house were the dollhouse Thoreau built for the Emerson girls out of a dresser which they called the "baby house," and the Aeolian harp.

An Aeolian harp is a wooden box the width of a window, about five inches deep, and an inch or two high. Three strings are strung lengthwise across the wooden box and attached to tuning pegs. The harp is placed on a window sill, strings up, and the wind rushing over the strings creates the music. Depending on the breeze, arpeggios or single tones from the harmonic series might sound. The music is organic and natural, but to the Transcendentalists the harp sound represented divinity in nature. That day was windless, so we didn't get to hear the harp, but Emerson gives a sense of its gentle sound in this poem:

Maiden Speech of the Aeolian Harp

Soft and softlier hold me, friends!
Thanks if your genial care
Unbind and give me to the air.
Keep your lips or finger-tips
For flute or spinet's dancing chips;
I await a tenderer touch,
I ask more or not so much:
Give me to the atmosphere,--
Where is the wind, my brother,--where?
Lift the sash, lay me within,
Lend me your ears, and I begin.
For gentle harp to gentle hearts
The secret of the world imparts;
And not to-day and not to-morrow
Can drain its wealth of hope and sorrow;
But day by day, to loving ear
Unlocks new sense and loftier cheer.
I've come to live with you, sweet friends,
This home my minstrel-journeying ends.
Many and subtle are my lays,
The latest better than the first,
For I can mend the happiest days
And charm the anguish of the worst.

Ralph Waldo Emerson

After the Emerson house visit, we saw another Aeolian harp at the Concord Museum. This harp was among Thoreau's things: his green desk from the Walden Pond cabin, his flute, a walking stick, and many early editions of his creative work. I needed to find out more about the Aeolian harp, so I hit the books, or rather, the scholarly databases. I found a classic example of scholarly discourse, or asynchronous conversation between scholars, on the importance of sound to Thoreau. Scholar Sherman Paul in *The New England Quarterly* (1949) mentions Norman Foerster's examination of Thoreau and sound in the latter's "Nature in American Literature" published in 1923. Paul discusses the whippoorwill, cricket, woodthrush, and telegraph wire as natural sound generators in Thoreau's writing. The cricket and birds announce the times of day or season. But telegraph wire? Paul never mentions the Aeolian harp as a window instrument, but he does compare vibrating telegraph wires to an Aeolian harp. The telegraph wire in wind works the same way as the harp. Paul quotes Thoreau's journal: "The human soul is a silent harp in God's quire, whose strings need only to be swept by the divine breath to chime in with the harmonies of creation." That's a fantastic statement but to even the most practical thinker it illustrates the role of the harp as a central image of natural divinity to Thoreau.

In 1964, a scholar named Paul O. Williams built upon Sherman Paul's work. In the journal *PMLA*, Williams wrote in a more down-to-earth style about Thoreau's poems written through inspired experience. Those inspirations for Thoreau were commonly mundane natural phenomena such as dawn, dew, mist, fog, plus the concepts of ascent and sound.* Fellow Transcendentalist Emerson frequently wrote via inspired experience, too, and often with the same inspirations as his buddy Thoreau. Williams also cites the inspirational telegraph wires, but by way of Thoreau's poem, "Rumors from an Aeolian Harp:"

> There is a vale which none have seen,
> Where foot of man has never been,
> Such as here lives with toil and strife,
> An anxious and a sinful life.
> There every virtue has its birth,
> Ere it descends upon the earth,
> And thither every deed returns,
> Which in the generous bosom burns.
>
> There love is warm, and youth is young,
> And poetry is yet unsung.
> For Virtue still adventures there,
> And freely breathes her native air.
>
> And ever, if you hearken well,
> You still may hear its vesper bell,
> And tread of high-souled men go by,
> Their thoughts conversing with the sky.

Henry David Thoreau

* Williams, Paul O. "The Concept of Inspiration in Thoreau's Poetry." PMLA, vol. 79, no. 4, 1964, pp. 466–472. JSTOR, www.jstor.org/stable/460752.

As I read these poems and articles on a blustery fall day months after our Concord visit, I could hear the music of the wind outside in the leaves which remain on the trees, accompanied by the sound of the crackly fallen leaves on the ground. There goes a posse of Canada geese honking as they fly south. This is what Thoreau is talking about, I suppose: there's a symphony out there composed by the approaching cold front. It's aleatoric music, meaning created by chance, similar to the Twentieth Century Avant-Garde musical creations I learned about in graduate school. Aeolian harp music is focused on nature, though, woodthrushes, owls, crows, vibrating harp strings, and maybe a distant train.

Back in my research, I found that scholar Kenneth W. Rhoads wrote specifically about Thoreau and music in *American Literature* (1974). Music was vital to Thoreau, Rhoads says, as the Transcendentalist frequently expresses his fondness for it and employs musical metaphors. I found this clever quote in Thoreau's Journal: "A slight sound at evening lifts me up by the ears, and makes life inexpressibly serene and grand. It may be in Uranus, or it may be in the shutter." Thoreau's perception of music ranges anywhere from "concrete sensory experience to abstract metaphysical concept" according to Rhoads (p. 314).* I'm in for another lofty intellectual discussion of Thoreau's

* Rhoads, Kenneth W. "Thoreau: The Ear and the Music." *American Literature*, vol. 46, no. 3, 1974, pp. 313–328. JSTOR, www.jstor.org/stable/2924412.

Inspiration and craft, I predicted, but I was rewarded. After a nod to previous scholar Sherman Paul (see, scholarship is like a conversation), Rhoads gets into yet another discussion of the Aeolian harp! It was a central image for Thoreau, Emerson, and most of the Romantic poets, too. Coleridge and Shelley penned their own Aeolian harp odes. Scholar Rhoads finally lets us in on the instrument's significance: besides its gentle dulcet tones and random harmonies, the harp bridges the concept of art music with the idea of music representing the mystical divinity in nature.

The Alcott family lived in Orchard House, not quite a mile further east on Lexington Road from Emerson's corner. We arrived after lunch in town and were immediately swept onto a tour starting in the kitchen. Before even entering the house, Audrey and I noticed the lilacs in bloom on either side of the front door, and the "little patch of garden" that author Louisa May Alcott mentions in *Little Men*. The Alcott sisters enjoyed nature and gardening and this little garden was planted as they would have had it. Gardens enhance the author-experience of a house. Pearl S. Buck's gardens are carefully tended by volunteer gardeners to show that she loved her gardens, especially the camellias which are still grown in the greenhouses connected to her office. When my friend Bill visited writer Vita Sackville-West's home in England I asked him to be on the lookout for ways the curators convey her personality. She was a poet and novelist, but also an important garden designer. When Bill returned from that trip he told me it is "all about the garden." The gardeners painstakingly recreate the lush English gardens as Sackville-West had them. The gardens were her passion, and visitors learn that by seeing the grounds preserved.

The Alcotts' garden was not on the scale of Vita Sackville-West's but we know from reading Louisa's books that they enjoyed it and they enjoyed the apple trees from which their Orchard House got its name. Louisa's older sister, Anna, (Meg in *Little Women*) purposely married during apple blossom time so the scent of the blooms would waft in through the open windows. The sisters appreciated nature in a wilder form, too, and frequently traveled the short distance to Walden Pond to visit Mr. Thoreau in his tiny cabin there. He taught them about the native plants and animals.

So here we were, two sisters visiting the legendary home of four fictional sisters based on their creator's own siblings. The parallels end there. While these sisters were close in age and grew up together, my sister and I were seventeen years apart with no siblings in-between. She was always a grown-up in my eyes. In fact, she married when I was four. Here at Orchard House our age difference faded away. *Little Women* connected us. We both loved the book and in fact, were both shepherded through it by the same mom, also a Louisa May Alcott fan from childhood.

The Alcott girls would have walked to Walden Pond, but we sisters drove the MINI there on Sunday morning. We inspected the replica of Thoreau's tiny cabin and walked around the pond contemplating the interconnectedness of Concord's historic people and events. This cabin copy is not where Thoreau had his, but instead by the parking lot so that visitors like us wouldn't miss it. There's a copy of his green desk in there along with a chair, bed, stove, and two windows. It's small, but not much smaller than my freshman year dorm room, and that room only had one window. Thoreau wrote *Walden* here, but not until he had completed *A Year on the Concord and Merrimack Rivers* about a trip he and his brother, John, took just before John died.

> I went to the woods because I wished to live deliberately, to front only the essential facts of life, and see if I could not learn what it had to teach, and not, when I came to die, to discover that I had not lived. I did not wish to live what was not life, living is so dear; nor did I wish to practice resignation, unless it was quite necessary. I wanted to live deep and suck out all the marrow of life.

> Henry David Thoreau in *Walden*

Walden Pond is a tranquil place. We walked around it, about 1.7 miles according to the man on-duty in the Walden bookstore. Another walker said, "It's not usually like this. The water level is very low. Usually there's only a thin strip of sand around the pond." We were surprised that on the side nearest the road there was a sandy beach big enough to accommodate 50-75 people. I could get comfortable here, most likely sitting on a beach chair with a Thoreau book. The rest of the pond's perimeter measured anywhere from three to ten feet wide. We saw fishermen on this 70-degree day, families, young people relaxing, and a couple of older men swimming in wet suits. I didn't see anyone writing there at Thoreau's favorite spot.

I wished I could switch to x-ray vision because of a story my friend Charlie told me. She was staying nearby with a college friend, and rode her bike to Walden Pond. One day she walked the perimeter as we did and suddenly noticed a pipe sticking out of the water. The pipe moved, and Charlie realized that the pipe was attached to a man. They struck up a conversation when the man exclaimed, "You should see what's down there! You won't believe it!" So Charlie borrowed his snorkel pipe and mask, and went into the pond in her clothes to have a look around. There she saw all kinds of nineteenth-century wagons and carriages as if Thoreau's precious Walden Pond had been some kind of nineteenth-century transportation dump. Charlie, a cultural anthropologist, was astonished. There were no snorkelers when Audrey and I were at the pond.

"Well, if I were going to build a tiny cabin this is where I would build it," I remarked. Audrey agreed this cove on the pond's north side would be the best spot. We did not know where Thoreau's cabin had actually been, but this cove was sheltered and peaceful and we learned later his cabin did sit near where we were standing. Trails lead to the site and concrete markers show exactly where the famous cabin stood. Over the years Thoreau fans have placed rocks there, and evidently there's a pile there now. Without a map we were oblivious to this—there are no signs at the pond.

I loved the pond and the Thoreau Society's Shop

at Walden Pond. I bought a tie-dyed green T-shirt with his face on it and the words "What Would Thoreau Do?" even though I had resolved to not add to my enormous T-shirt collection. An exception was made for HD Thoreau since I was feeling very connected to him that day at "his" pond. I bought one of those oval stickers people put on their cars although I swore the new MINI would have none of that. I was falling in love with Thoreau although I realize he won't be an attentive beau. *I'll* always have to visit *him*, for example, but I think I will be delighted to do that six-hour drive as long as Walden Pond is waiting for me at the end.

Next, the Old Manse, Waldo Emerson's grandfather's house. William Emerson was a minister in the eighteenth century and lived here with his wife and children. They were living here when a battle took place at a little bridge outside a bedroom window. Mrs. Emerson watched the battle that would be the first of the American Revolution and which her grandson Waldo would call "The shot heard 'round the world" in his poem, "Concord Hymn."

Waldo Emerson lived in this house sixty years after the Reverend Emerson. In this very same bedroom he wrote *Nature*, a transformative, Transcendentalist essay. He had his desk positioned near that very same window which looks out upon the famous North Bridge (now Minute Man National Park). He found the scene inspiring, but ten years later another resident of this house, renter Nathaniel Hawthorne, found the scene distracting and built himself a little desk attached to the opposite wall. He wrote *Mosses from an Old Manse* with his back to the window. (I bought a copy at the

Manse's book shop and longed to sit under a big tree there to read it.) Hawthorne and his wife were a romantic couple, probably annoyingly "romantic," and used her diamond ring to etch love notes to each other in the glass of two of the windows in this room. A century and a half later we could still read some of their etchings.

Back downstairs in the ladies' drawing room, on a table draped with a delicate white cloth we found the third Aeolian harp of Concord! The window was shut so there was no wind moving over the strings. I doubt there was any wind that day, either. Later, in the book shop, I was happy to see a compact disc of Aeolian harp music and learn that my new love Thoreau crafted Aeolian harps and revised the design by replacing the sides with blocks meant for the window to sit on. This would amplify the vibrations of the strings through the wood of the harp to the window frame. Thoreau made the divine music louder.

A Steinway square grand piano sat in the corner of the men's drawing room, and we were invited to play it. We weren't allowed to touch anything or sit on the chairs, but we could play the piano?! (I did, but it wasn't memorable for anyone but me.) Usually, pianos in historic homes are off-limits. Johann Strauss II's piano in his Vienna home is in a glass box, and Mozart's is set far away from any visitor's path. You can't go near Elvis's piano at Graceland, but visitors pass a little closer to his electronic organ that we were told he played on the morning of the day he died. Those men are all musicians, but even at other writers' houses you wouldn't expect to touch the keyboards.

Pearl S. Buck's house contains a large organ, but there's no way a visitor could go near it. And then there's Beth Alcott's melodeon at Orchard House: keep your fingers off that!

In Concord, Emerson's house, the Old Manse, and the Alcotts' Orchard House were all occupied by family members into the twentieth century and then almost immediately transformed into museums. Curators did not have to search for furnishings "of the time" to approximate what a room would look like (as in Mozart's *Figarohaus*) because the family items were still in place. This was the case in Elvis's Graceland and Pearl S. Buck's Green Hills Farm, too. These family-owned artifacts add to the authenticity of the experience but they add some thrilling magic, too: a writer's desk, a musician's piano, clothing, original art.

I got to tour Louis Armstrong's house in Queens, New York, with a group of music librarians before it was ready to open to the public and I raved about that experience for months. I got to see his closet, every surface of which was covered with wallpaper, even the insides of the built-in drawers. The closet poles were hung very high and Louis was not a tall man. Each hanger had its own stick attached so that he could bring down the suit he wished to wear. We got to stand in his study where he practiced and sometimes walked out on the balcony to give impromptu concerts for the neighborhood kids. I remember shelves loaded with boxes of reel-to-reel tapes. Armstrong taped himself when he practiced the trumpet and kept the tapes. Our guide showed us that Armstrong had decorated each tape box, découpage-style, with magazine clippings and other bits of paper. Whenever I hear a Louis Armstrong song now, I think of standing on that hallowed ground and discovering these personal things about the man.

I had that feeling again when I stood transfixed in Louisa May Alcott's bedroom. There was the little "half-moon" desk that her father Bronson made for her, attached to the wall between two windows facing Lexington Road. It was just a ledge, really. Above the desk was a narrow strip of calla lilies with a black background painted on the wall by her younger sister May to cheer Louisa when she was bedridden with typhoid fever for many months. We toured the home in the month of May, so older sister Anna's (Meg in the book) brown silk wedding dress was displayed on the bed. The curators display it in May because Anna Alcott married John Bridge Pratt in the downstairs parlor in May when the orchard's apple blossoms were in bloom. The family was poor, but when Louisa started selling her writing and seeing royalties she bought things for the family home. We saw the expensive soapstone sink she bought for the kitchen and imagined how that would have improved the quality of daily life exponentially. I expect that many of the items I saw will come to mind as I read more of Alcott's works or re-read *Little Women*.

Our Orchard House tour guide asked us early on if we preferred book names (Meg-Jo-Beth-Amy) or real names (Anna-Louisa-Beth-May). I don't remember what we said, but she switched back and forth so that Meg was called Meg and sometimes Anna, and May was more often Amy. Although *Little Women* is set in

Orchard House, we learned that Beth never lived there. She died of scarlet fever before the family moved in, but they installed her melodeon with a picture of Beth over it as a memorial. The sisters were devoted to each other, to their mother ("Marmee"), and to neighbors and friends in Concord. Beth caught scarlet fever when she visited an afflicted family with Marmee. Visiting Orchard House was a "dream fulfilled" as my sister said, and the highlight of our Concord trip.

Many years ago, I was in Prince Edward Island, Canada, and visited the *Anne of Green Gables* sites with my then-husband. The house *Green Gables* was modeled on was there, and author LM Montgomery's house was nearby. We visited both of those and one of the guides gave us directions to LM Montgomery's grave. "You won't be able to miss it," she said, "there's a path worn in the grass leading up to it."

Why would I want to visit her *grave*? We went anyway. At her plot I was overcome with the sensation that this person was real, and although her books live on, she as a mortal person passed away as all people do. Her remains were in the ground under my feet, and how many others must have paid respects here. *Thank you for your art, your creation: that imaginary world with its beloved people,* I thought. I never pass up a chance to visit an author's or musician's grave now. I visit Pearl S. Buck's whenever I go to Green Hills Farm, and I visited JS Bach's in Leipzig. Elvis Presley is buried with his parents at Graceland, and visitors walk a path right by them. This was a moving experience for me and I found myself immobilized just staring at that charismatic performer's final resting place. How long did I stand there, I wonder?

It will be no surprise then, that Audrey and I left a visit to the Sleepy Hollow Cemetery in Concord for last. It would be the big finish for our Concord experience. Emerson, Thoreau, Alcott, Hawthorne, their spouses and families, and even Margaret Sidney, the author of *Five Little Peppers and How They Grew* are buried at Author's Ridge in this cemetery. (I still feel guilt over not letting my father read *Five Little Peppers* to me as a kid. Why did I hate that book so much? Was it outdated? Did I not approve of the old-fashioned line-drawn picture of unmodern kids on its cover?)

At Author's Ridge, we found Henry David Thoreau's grave first. Someone left him a pine cone, and many left small stones. We discovered that the *thing to do here* is to leave pens and pencils for the authors. Thoreau had a tidy pile. The Alcotts rest next to the Thoreaus, and Louisa has an even bigger pile of writing utensils. She will not run out of ink or lead in the afterlife. There was a long-stemmed red rose lying across her marble marker. (I wish I had thought to bring trinkets for the authors.) There were many Emersons at Author's Ridge. Waldo's marker is hard to miss: he has a boulder of rose quartz with a patina'd plate on it. A few steps away, the romantic Hawthornes rested in the shade. He had his own collection of pens and pencils.

Gazing upon these graves I was struck by the same feeling of reverence that I caught at Elvis's, LM Montgomery's, and Pearl S. Buck's graves. These were real people who walked the same earth I do. It was there, at Author's Ridge, that I realized how linked this

Transcendentalist community was in life and even in death. I felt connected to the real Alcott, Emerson, Thoreau, and even Hawthorne by visiting their homes, but the sum of these Concord residences gave me a deeper understanding of this group of like-minded, original-thinking friends and their connections.

I wasn't interested in Transcendentalism when I went to Concord. What started as a pilgrimage to a favorite childhood author's famous home turned into a transcendental, and Transcendental, exploration of the community in which Louisa May Alcott lived. Isn't that the most memorable kind of travel? I stumbled upon Thoreau and Emerson and recognized them as kindred spirits. Emerson was the abstract Transcendental thinker, and Thoreau applied these ideas to living. Both valued the personal divinity of the individual, self-reliance, individualism, and the importance of books as I have always. They stretched their curiosity beyond their young country to Ancient Greek and Hindu writings. They were misunderstood for their ideas and beliefs as I have been. For them, misunderstanding was actually part of the solution to a problem. They tied up these concepts for me in a tidy compact package, didn't they? I see myself in this constellation of ideas. Now if I can just remember: Misunderstanding is part of the solution!

There are still marvelous discoveries to make—was I arrogant to think I had already discovered everything I might find interesting? The Transcendentalists have communicated with my being, and shown me a whole new world of original thought for me to explore.

Riding the Silver
Eagle South

Books must be read as deliberately and
reservedly as they are written.

~Henry David Thoreau, *Walden* (1854)

My life is like a stroll on the beach,
As near the ocean's edge as I can go.

~Henry David Thoreau, "The Fisher's Boy" (1849)

I hate quotations. Tell me what you know.

~Ralph Waldo Emerson's Journal (1849)

Riding the Silver People Snake

Trains, cars, boats, subway, bridges, and inclines: Pittsburgh is a transportation city.

The long, silver people-snake slowly slithered into Trenton, and that's where I embarked upon this journey. I splurged on a Business Class seat on the Amtrak "Pennsylvanian," which is a nice touch when you have luggage and the idea that you would like to read and write while the scenery changes outside your window for eight hours. My expectation was that there would be scenery outside and people-watching drama inside. (Maybe I would find scenery inside and drama outside?) The Spanish have a word for travel when the experience is more important than the destination: *vacilando*. In my case, the journey was as important as the destination, and ultimately the two would blend to form my story.

I was excited about this railroad journey and I was overthinking it, as usual. I was headed to my favorite librarian conference, which is focused on those of us who provide online reference, instruction, and other library services to virtual-campus students at colleges and universities. Every minute of the conference would be relevant and worthwhile for my job, and this year I would enjoy the added bonus of spending time with a close friend from my freshman year of college at Duquesne University in Pittsburgh.

I'm well-acquainted with the scenery outside the train between Trenton and Philadelphia, so for that leg of the journey I ignored the outside scenery and explored my little piece of train. I had a reclining seat, a curtain, outlets to save battery power on my devices, and a handy tray table similar to an airplane's but bigger. The restrooms were in front, and the snack car was behind me. I could be comfortable here all day, I thought. In Philadelphia's 30th Street Station, my railroad workspace was plunged into darkness without warning while the train consist (a railroader's word for string of cars) was outfitted with a diesel locomotive for the rest of the trip. From New York through Newark and Trenton, New Jersey, and then to Philadelphia, the people snake was powered by an electric locomotive because diesels and the fumes they produce are not allowed in the underground tunnels of New York. Between Philadelphia and Pittsburgh we would be powered by a diesel locomotive. This bit of information is courtesy of the older man behind me in the green jacket who provided commentary all the way to Pittsburgh except when he was watching movies without the benefit of headphones.

After approximately 20 minutes of darkness in 30th Street Station, we were on our way west. I was settling in with a Paul Theroux book (*Last Train to Zona Verde*, 2013) about his most recent trip in Africa when an elderly gentleman in a yellow shirt with a blood-soaked sleeve was escorted to a seat across the aisle from me. He had fallen down the escalator in the Philadelphia station and cut his arm. There was quite a bit of blood, but he seemed lucid and unfazed. That situation could have been so much worse. He accepted first aid from train personnel, but did not wish to go to the hospital. He was travelling all the way to Pittsburgh, so the conductor advised him he could get off at any point if he changed his mind about seeking medical attention. A report was written and he signed it. He did not know I was writing about him, and he did not know I'd be watching over him. (I have spent a good part of my life looking out for older adults, so when one gets hurt I feel for them.) My hero travel writer, Paul Theroux, often reminds his readers that one of the perks of writing on a train is that people can't catch you writing about them. The yellow-shirted injured man did not supply any more drama—he seemed to be okay.

While the injured-man drama was happening on the train, I was keeping an eye on the changing scenery out my window. There was a cliff or bluff next to the multiple tracks, and atop the cliff were old-fashioned 19th-century rowhouses. The residents must have been throwing large trash items over that cliff for decades: there were mattresses, furniture, used bricks, and other scraps of city life forming a potential urban archeology study a few yards from the outermost track. Farther west in the suburbs, properties were more carefully manicured, but many butted-up against the tracks and others sat on top of cliffs as in the city.

Paoli, Exton, Lancaster…

Who is this guy who wears a retroactively-fashionable feathered hat and walks up and down the aisle as if he owns the train? He located the first aid kit for the injured man, so maybe he does have something to do with the train. By Altoona, he will have stripped-down to a sleeveless T-shirt and switched to a "newsboy" hat, but still walked the aisle as if he had something to do with the operation of the train. I considered asking him, but what if, I thought, what if he is an undercover railroad policeman and my question ruined his cover? This was a mystery I would not solve.

The scenes became rural as we approached Lancaster County, about two hours west of Philadelphia. There were fields of propane tanks, trees, dirt, broken concrete, my own reflection, houses with green grass, churches, graveyards, farms, plowed fields and fields being plowed. In Lancaster County, Amish Country, there were big, two-story, chunky, square, brick houses with big porches of which I was jealous, and nicely-tended green lawns. Many lawns featured trampolines. I saw ball fields, farms, silos, cows, sheep, horses, a labyrinth made of stones outside a church, quilts displayed for purchase, and a plow drawn by five horses - or were they mules?

"It is a feeling of utter quietness, deep rural isolation the train briefly penetrates." That's Paul Theroux musing about 1970s Yugoslavia in his earlier book, *The Great Railway Bazaar* (1975), but he could have been writing about Lancaster. This is where many Pennsylvania Dutch (Amish, Mennonite, and others) live in various states of off-the-grid for religious reasons. Farming is the main industry here, but canning (or "putting-up") the resulting produce, hand quilting, baking, and gardening are evident to the visitor. I drive here often for the best prices and selection on good quality cotton quilting fabric sold to me by friendly women with sheer white caps pinned to their hair buns. They are probably Mennonites because they operate cash registers. The Amish stay away from electricity except for the occasional generator-supplied kind. When I drive to Lancaster County on a fabric-buying mission, I'm mostly surrounded by the other local industry, tourism: smorgasbords, quilts, hotels, shops, and even a Pennsylvania-Dutch-themed amusement park. A wrong turn could put you in a "deep rural isolation" similar to that which Theroux found in Yugoslavia, or at least I imagine it that way. The train tracks, however, provide a different perspective from the highways: truly rural without the tourism.

Mount Joy, Elizabethtown, Harrisburg…

It was near Harrisburg, Pennsylvania's state capital, that the quiet older woman in front of me appeared in my personal train-space to announce that she had dropped her hearing aid and she surmised that it was probably on the floor near my seat. I crawled around and looked under the seats, and shined my smartphone flashlight around, but there was no hearing aid. I suggested that maybe it fell between the armrest and wall and got stuck in there. During the brief stop in Harrisburg, she got the conductor to help, and explained that this nice lady (me) had been kind enough to look on the floor, but the hearing aid wasn't there. He had the same thought I did, but went a step further and turned her seat away from the wall revealing a kind of tray under the armrest. There sat the hearing aid. I picked it up and handed it to the woman standing out of the way in the aisle while the conductor held her seat sideways. "That's $1900 saved," said the woman, and I considered myself a hero even though I guess the conductor who turned the seat rightfully gets the save.

Susquehanna, Lewistown, Huntingdon…

After Harrisburg we moved on over the Susquehanna River (so said the man in the green jacket behind me, but I already suspected that was the Susquehanna). Then came Lewistown with its picturesque train station and Americana town. From the train I saw the Shy Beaver Boat Center, a bowling alley, lots of train tracks, and a city hall with an aesthetically-pleasing clock tower. There was a man in a striped shirt and overalls waiting for someone to appear from inside the modern people snake, and he'd probably bring this person back to his typical Lewistown farmhouse or perhaps one of those log cabins further outside the town. As we left Lewistown, I noticed what I thought were trainspotters with cameras, but I would learn later this is not what they are called.

A brief stop in Huntingdon, PA: the Thompson Candle Co, A Christmas Shoppe, Sherwin-Williams, The Uniform Place, Victorian buildings with mansard roofs, a factory with smokestacks, a church steeple with a clock. "Herein, I think, is the chief attraction of railway travel. The speed is so easy, and the train disturbs so little the scenes which it takes us, that our heart becomes full of the placidity and stillness of the country…" That's Paul Theroux again describing my trip by musing about his own in *The Great Railway Bazaar*. I actually saved money by taking the train, not to mention gas and effort, and I was delighted by the scenery outside and captivated by the drama inside. I wasn't getting much reading in, so Theroux would have to wait in Africa until I had some undistracted time to follow him on that journey. I was entranced by my own.

While the guy behind me watched a movie on his iPad without headphones, I began to listen to my audio book with my noise-reducing headphones. This did not last long because I realized I missed too much aurally. The train stopped. I heard only the tail-end of the announcement: "...trespasser on the tracks was injured...probably a dirt biker. We're waiting for the mess to be cleared up." The "mess?!" Oh my. Now we are having a drama outside the train. After a half-hour the train began to move again. About a mile from where we stopped I saw a fire engine and ambulance with emergency lights flashing right near the tracks. What kind of "mess" did they have to clean up, I wondered.

Tyrone, Altoona, Johnstown...

"Watch your step detraining in Altoona!" It's more industrial here, and Altoona has its own transit center with lots of train tracks leading to it. It was late afternoon by then and the light had changed the interior train scenery. My reflection in the window glass was now clearer. There I am with Pennsylvania's changing landscape as my backdrop. I saw more photographers trackside and wondered what they were trying to capture. There's nothing unusual about this train, I thought. Back at work, I asked my librarian colleague, Brian, a railroad expert, about those guys with cameras. I made the mistake of calling them trainspotters. "First of all, there is no such thing as trainspotting in this country," he told me. "We're railfans and we're railfanning." Brian told me those photographers/ railfans were probably out there shooting every train that went by, both freight and passenger. "They wouldn't ignore what you think are ordinary Amtrak trains because the color schemes change and someday this scheme will be interesting." Railfans are especially interested in freight trains and the types of cars making up the "consist." Intermodal trains have mixed cars: containers, tractor trailers, tankers, etc. Unit trains have all the same kind of cars.

As we chugged along, I started to get drowsy. This trip takes about eight hours and I didn't want to snooze because I would miss something interesting. I wanted a nap, but then the conductor was announcing the famous Horseshoe Curve, a marvel of modern railroading at Kittaning Point near the Allegheny Mountains. It didn't matter that I'd seen it before, twice. It was breathtaking to contemplate this tight hairpin railroad curve which opened way back in February 1854. An engineer named J. Edgar Thompson designed it, and his plans were realized by mostly Irish workers who were paid 25 cents per day to build it by hand. The central angle of the curve is 220 degrees which to non-engineers means that you can see almost all of your train's exterior by looking out your window while on the curve. I didn't realize until just now when I looked up the Curve's details that while the train is navigating the tight curve it is also climbing 122 feet going from east to west. I'll have to remember to sit on the other side of the train for a better view when I go home… okay, it'll be the same side when the train turns around. I'm glad I thought that through.

Just after the Horseshoe Curve, the engineer hurled the silver people snake into a hole in the side of a mountain. We were in a tunnel, of course, in total darkness with "NO SIGNAL" showing on my phone. As long as we kept moving I wasn't concerned, but I can imagine some claustrophobics might be a little nervous at this point. There I am again, in the window glass which has become a mirror with a black background. Should I distract you from the dark tunnel with the story of where I first heard a train referred to as a "people snake?" Around thirty years ago at Temple University in Philadelphia, my friend Vince and I were headed for the Broad Street Subway. There was a young man in distress, probably from drugs, or maybe from a psychological issue, and he repeatedly screamed, "The people snake! The people snake!" He was being assisted by law enforcement professionals, so Vince and I walked on and entered the subway. We looked at each other and delightedly mouthed the words "people snake!" Ever since then I am reminded of that man and his creative imagery whenever I see a train slither by. I've never used the image until now, but I never forgot that vivid urban scene. It's almost as if I've been saving the "people snake" for this story.

Latrobe, Greensburg, Pittsburgh…

The sunlight was golden when we emerged from the tunnel, making everything look lovely, even that school bus parking lot. There are natural scenes out there, too: streams, hills, and a river far below train level. The houses on the hills surrounding us are mostly brick, and suddenly, look: we're in the city of Pittsburgh. The stately old train station is still there, but Amtrak uses only a small, ugly back portion of it. This is the end of the line for the Pennsylvanian. There's a cab stand outside the door, and I relaxed on the short ride to the William Penn Hotel, one of the few Downtown landmarks I remember from that long-ago freshman year in this city. The library conference would start the next afternoon, so for now I was free to settle in to this comfortable room: hang up my clothes, put on my pajamas, and look for something good on TV. I'm not sure why I had two bathrooms, two closets, and all that extra floor space, but the feeling of having more than you need is a delicious pleasure.

I'll sum up the conference like this: it was successful, satisfying and fulfilling. I took lots of notes in my little notebook, and saw librarian friends I typically see only at this conference which takes place every two years in a different city. I got to see parts of the William Penn Hotel that the typical guest doesn't see: presentations in the meeting rooms, poster sessions in the fabulous Art Deco Urban Room, and breakfasts and lunches in the magnificent ballroom where Lawrence Welk and his orchestra performed and invented his innovative bubble-making machine. (My younger colleagues had no idea why I was so excited that the original bubble machine was displayed in the lobby.) It is consistently a good conference and I would return to work with some new ideas.

Do you ever wonder if, as on TV, this whole adult thing is just a dream and we could wake up one day to find ourselves back in time? It famously happened to Bob Newhart on his sitcom's finale and to Pam Ewing on *Dallas*. What if I woke up back in my tiny freshman dorm room at Duquesne University? There would be mean old Geraldine, my first roommate. Daryl Hall and John Oates would be on the radio singing "Private Eyes" and "I Can't Go for That" for the three-thousandth time this week, and Joan Jett and the Blackhearts would be singing about how much they love Rock and Roll. At some point that year, I saw *Raiders of the Lost Ark* in the movie theater. Ronald Reagan was president. Jeanne and Karen were my closest friends, the last survivors from a bigger group of freshman girls who got together on Friday evenings to eat pizza and watch *Dynasty* and *Falcon Crest* on television. One-by-one they found other, more adventurous, friends and boyfriends and left our little pizza group.

I was in turmoil that year, extremely homesick and writing letters to my mom who was stuck at home caring for my dad, trying his best to recover from a stroke. I missed my boyfriend, Rob, terribly and wrote him, too. There was no email yet and long-distance phone calls were expensive. I was unhappy with the major I thought I wanted since I started playing the clarinet at age ten. I signed up to study Music Education, but once I was there, I realized I wanted to study Music Theory, but I'd have to transfer somewhere else to get that major. I built a bridge over that troubled water by spending long hours playing the clarinet and spending time with friends: Backgammon with Karen and Pittsburgh explorations with Jeanne.

As far as I can tell, this adult life is real, and after the conference I was looking forward to exploring Pittsburgh with Jeanne thirty-plus years after that freshman year. She was anxious to show me around Pittsburgh's new attractions, and I was anxious to see what New Pittsburgh had to offer. As fate would have it, I was experiencing some emotional turmoil in this city. My beautiful, long-haired cat, Honey, had passed away the week before at age twelve, leaving a hole in the fabric of our household. On the one hand, I wanted to stay home under a quilt and grieve; on the other hand a change of scenery was a healthy choice. On top of that, it was in one of those conference rooms that I found out through social media Prince had died. Back at Temple University after I transferred from Duquesne, I wore out my cassette tape of the soundtrack to Prince's *Purple Rain*. My roommate, JoAnne, did not appreciate that music so much. She preferred my other non-classical cassette tape, the soundtrack to Barbra Streisand's *Yentl*. According to our dorm neighbors, she cranked the volume on that when I was away, and one day the tape snapped from sheer exhaustion. The loss of Honey the cat in 2016 compounded by the sudden death of Prince recalled the angst I suffered during that long-ago freshman year. Once again, it would be Jeanne who cheered me up.

In the winter and early spring of that freshman year, the same group who ordered pizza delivery on Friday evenings would step out to explore Pittsburgh. The group dwindled as its members found other interests, and only Jeanne and I remained loyal to our explorations by the end of the academic year. I felt like I was back in college while riding around with Jeanne discovering new landmarks and attractions and forming a bigger mental map of the city *because we had a car.* The college illusion was made authentic by the underlying sadness I felt, this time not homesickness but the grief of losing Honey and Prince.

We have stayed in touch for over thirty years, first by handwritten letters, then occasionally word-processed snail mail, and then we eventually switched to email. We're both on Facebook now, and during my stay in Pittsburgh we graduated to texting. It's a cliché to say it, but when we reunite in person we pick up where we left off as good old friends do. My mental map of the city, except for its shape and some street names, is lost. During breaks from the conference I had to navigate like a first-time visitor, so I was glad when she joined me for the post-conference playtime. She seemed to know what would interest me.

Pittsburgh transformed into a 21st century city while I wasn't looking. Rather than attempting to exist on its steel and coal mining history, Pittsburgh now accentuates its positives: transportation, rivers, bridges, a new casino, and Andy Warhol. The grand big-city department stores we suburban-mall-cultured college girls shopped in during the 1980s are gone, and in their place are restaurants, parks, plazas, and new modern skyscrapers. There's even a plaza lined with restaurants where we spent our first dinner. NOLA on the Square is a New Orleans themed restaurant where I had beignets that could have come straight from Café du Monde in New Orleans, except that they came with a side of cotton candy ice cream.

To get to the Andy Warhol Museum, we drove over what used to be called the Seventh Street Bridge but is now officially the Andy Warhol Bridge. It is one of three identical yellow bridges known as the Three Sisters which connect Downtown with the North Shore over the Allegheny River: the Roberto Clemente Bridge, the Andy Warhol, and the Rachel Carson. The Andy Warhol Museum is on the North Shore, a few blocks from the bridge. I think I could have walked here had it been open when I was at Duquesne—what a treat it would have been then! I would have found solace there. Alas, it didn't open in the repurposed Frick-Lindsay Building until 1994, well after my Pittsburgh departure.

The Andy Warhol Museum experience begins on the top floor and visitors descend as the exhibits follow chronologically. Jeanne and I were engrossed in the exhibit on Warhol's early life in Pittsburgh and his student art before we got to the famous, colorful celebrity (Marilyn Monroe) and consumer product art (Campbell's Soup and Brillo pads). Reproductions of these are ubiquitous, but here are the originals! There are 900 paintings and 100 sculptures in this collection, 2000 works on paper and 1000 prints. This is worldwide Warhol scholarship headquarters. Pop Art is happy art, except when it isn't. After taking in the more serious and gritty art from Warhol's later years, we were hungry, and decided to visit another one of Pittsburgh's attractions, the 2009 Rivers Casino.

I tried to count how many bridges we crossed en route, but this was an impossible task. Pittsburgh's Downtown is at the point where three rivers converge: the Allegheny, the Monongahela, and the Ohio. Traffic flows constantly over the many bridges as people go from the North Shore to Downtown and the South

Side, and to eastern sections with names like Oakland, Squirrel Hill, and Morningside. Rivers Casino is on the North Shore, kind of, but far enough to the west that it looks out on the Ohio River rather than the Allegheny River under the Warhol Bridge. The views from the casino are worth the trip. We could see The Point, the location where the three rivers come together (also called The Confluence), and the skyscrapers of Downtown behind The Point. We could see Mount Washington on the South Side and the inclines we would ride the next day. We could see the bridges connecting the South Side with Downtown over the Monongahela River and some tourist boats travelling under the bridges. We're not gamblers, so we enjoyed the River Walk outside the busy casino after our dinner at the buffet. Pittsburgh has sure changed, but yeah, we have, too.

An accidental theme for this trip was starting to emerge: Transportation and how it unifies and connects the city. I had no concept of this back in the 1980s.. We had planned for weeks to go on one of those amphibious truck/boat tours and then ride the incline up steep Mount Washington on the South Side. The "Duck Boat" tour was more thorough than we expected, taking us through Downtown past the William Penn Hotel and the skyscrapers, the parks and the plazas, and then plunging into the Monongahela River. The driver and the tour guide kept us laughing—

hard—throughout the tour. We saw the sites from the water, drifting close to The Point where a groundhog was frolicking on the concrete surrounding the fountain. (Where did he come from?) We rode over near Rivers Casino where we could see the Mister (Fred) Rogers statue. (He is one of Pittsburgh's favorite sons, and his wife who supplied the theme music for his public TV show played a recital at Duquesne while I was there. None other than Fred Rogers himself showed up in the audience and I missed it!) Our Duck Boat tour left us at our starting point at Station Square, which is a transportation hub. The city's light rail train (the "T") stops there, freight trains roll through, and many tourist boats start from there. We watched a freight train roll through with many curious-looking cars, all the same, in its consist (a unit train). They turned out to be automobile haulers.

Aross the street and down a block we found the Monongahela Incline's Lower Station. This funicular takes passengers up and down steep Mount Washington. For locals, it's just a piece of a commute but for tourists it is a unique experience to look out the window at the very steep slope from the inside of these ancient funicular cars. The cars are balanced: when one goes up, another comes down. Pittsburgh has only two of these inclines left, but there used to be 17. The Monongahela Incline was built in 1870 to take residents, about 15 per car, from the top of Mount Washington to the bottom where they could transfer to other modes of transportation like the buses and the light rail to cross the Monongahela River or walk across the Smithfield Bridge.

I remember Jeanne and I rode the other incline back in those college days. Back then we had our whole adult lives in front of us and our big life questions were: Who will we marry? Where would we settle? What would our careers be? On this trip the life questions left unanswered were more like: Will I stay in this position until I retire? When will I retire? Where will I live? Is this all there is?

The Incline took us to the top of Mount Washington where we stood on one of many lookouts and gazed upon the city. What struck me in this fantastic view was the movement: freight trains, light rail trains (the "T") on the Panhandle Bridge, boats, and vehicles on the many other bridges: perpetual motion. From this vantage point one can clearly see that Pittsburgh's bridges are painted one of three colors: black, blue, or yellow (officially Aztec Gold). These are Pittsburgh's official colors, based on William Pitt's shield according to the Duck Boat guide. Watching the city move, I thought about the average college student or professional commuter making Theroux-like connections: take the Incline to the bottom of the mountain, catch the "T" to Downtown, and then maybe a bus to campus or office. How mundane it must seem if you do it every day, but to me it seems like an adventure, a transportation puzzle, constantly moving and connecting.

Later that day, I found myself standing on another overlook, this time it was Jeanne's deck built on a steep hill covered with wildflowers and trees. I remember her telling me about having this structure built in a long-ago letter. The scene was tranquil and seemed remote from the busy city which was only about fifteen minutes away by car. We sat and talked and played with Oreo, her canine roommate. I didn't want to go back to the hotel because that would mean my Pittsburgh visit was almost over. It is great for the soul reconnecting with an old friend.

I had another eight-hour train ride to look forward to. This time, I read more, following Paul Theroux on his African trip in *Last Train to Zona Verde*. In this book Theroux combines train travel with other modes as he travels through three countries in Africa. He muses on the effect aging has on his travel now, and the flavor of the tale is more somber than my other Theroux train favorites, *The Great Railway Bazaar* (1975), *The Old Patagonian Express* (1979), and *Riding the Iron Rooster* (1988). He was a younger, stronger, more optimistic traveler in those. He writes best about train travel, weaving mini-interviews with passengers with observations on the landscape outside his window. It seemed that every time I looked up from the book there was a long freight train blocking the view of my scenery. When I saw a freight train being pulled by four locomotives, I was compelled to count the cars: 86! I enjoyed the view from this side of the train: little towns with clock towers and churches, more railfans, and lots of trees and babbling brooks.

This trip was different. After so many airplane excursions, I actually felt like I had traveled the distance between Trenton, NJ, and Pittsburgh, PA. I watched the scenery change and I had the feeling of being in constant motion, even while at my destination. The train was the perfect mode of travel for visiting Pittsburgh. I was part of this huge, intricate, extended transportation system that so entranced me while I stood at the top of Mount Washington. At the same time there was the theme of age: Jeanne and I are middle-aged homeowners now instead of teenaged college girls, Pittsburgh has modernized, and Paul Theroux is concerned about adventurous train travel at his advanced age. "Time and tide wait for no man," and neither do the cars, the boats, the buses, the inclines, the people snakes, and age.

Celebrating Schubert's Art Songs with St. Petersburg Tea

What concert hall has more history than Andrew Carnegie's Carnegie Hall? This day was for Franz Schubert and the Russian Tea Room next door.

Carnegie Hall robo-called me the day before: "Please arrive early for this event. The performance will have no intermission and there will be no late seating." I was terribly worried that something would make me late. I rode the New Jersey Transit Northeast Corridor commuter train to New York's Penn Station, walked north to 57th Street and turned right where I would find the legendary Carnegie Hall and the Russian Tea Room beside it. It was cool enough to debut the thick wool Aran sweater I had purchased in Dublin, but at the same time was sunny and pleasant for a walk through crowded Times Square, past the carts with fragrant roasted chestnuts for sale, past the vendors selling designer handbag knock-offs and faux pashminas, and into the Carnegie Hall neighborhood. There would be a lot of walking today, notably mine and that of the protagonist/traveler in Schubert's *Winterreise*.

Winterreise, a song cycle based on poems by Wilhelm Müller, was composed late in Franz Schubert's brief life. (A song cycle is usually a set of linked songs based on existing poetry. Usually the songs are set for voice with piano accompaniment.) Schubert knew he was dying by the time he was creating *Winterreise* and chose Müller's group of poems written from the point of view of a weary traveler to represent his own wretched sorrow. Although gloomy, these poems inspired Schubert to compose an innovative song cycle, one where the piano part is elevated to the importance of the voice. In other words, the piano is not mere accompaniment but contributes its own melodic material to the piece.

Winterreise has been an important part of my musical life. Studying the cycle in graduate school led to an epiphany. Up until this point I had synthesized what I was learning about a composer and his cultural milieu to inform the pieces of serious art music ("classical" music) I would hear in class. I had avoided any kind of vocal or choral music because of my lack of singing talent and avoidance of choir singing. I was a clarinetist and preferred instrumental music. However, in Professor Epstein's seminar I was learning to appreciate the words in a piece of music and their influence on a composer's musical choices. This was big. It gave me insight into how to think about and interpret opera, choral sections of orchestral music (Beethoven's Ninth Symphony!), and of course art songs. It was as if a whole new world of music had opened up to me. I really didn't like Professor Epstein due to his lack of a sense of humor, truth be told, but I'm grateful for this musical experience.

CARNEGIE HALL

There it was, the boxy, unmistakable, revered tan-brick concert hall that Andrew Carnegie built for his wife Louise's choral society. I scrutinized the façade: strange that a concert hall would have so many windows, but perhaps those were offices and studios in front. The fire escape on the Seventh Avenue side was painted tan to match the bricks. All around the fire escape were windows that seemed to be bricked-up, but on second thought were probably just architectural elements to echo the actual windows in the front. The top level, heavily windowed, is set in from the other three-quarters of the building like an upper layer on a square wedding cake. Three flags flew above the main entrance: an American flag flanked by two quadrilateral (but not rectangular) white banners bearing the 21st-century Carnegie Hall logo, primarily a giant red "C." Just beyond the venue stands the sixteen-story Carnegie Hall Tower where music lessons are taught to prodigies and professionals and where I would find the Rose Museum and Shop at Carnegie Hall. These would be my reward for allowing ample time to get to the concert.

I walked past the front of the edifice straining to see inside the darkened lobby when suddenly I was staring at the Russian Tea Room. I didn't realize it is practically next-door to Carnegie Hall. I had about an hour to kill before the restaurant opened at 11:00, so I walked around this vaguely familiar neighborhood. On Sundays, the little shops are closed, except for one tiny Christmas shop on Seventh Avenue. I went in only to find most of the customer floor space taken up by a rather large stroller which was not going to have enough room to even turn around in there. I gave the ornaments and Christmas trinkets a once-over, smiled at the woman at the counter, and fled before the young parents realized they'd have to back the gargantuan stroller out of the tiny store. A few other customers would have to be rearranged for this to happen.

THE RUSSIAN TEA ROOM

At 11:00 sharp I entered the Russian Tea Room

('RTR' on its logos), and my senses became overloaded. The room's dark green walls were covered with gold-framed oil paintings, and the authentic Russian waiter (from Gorky) led me across a green patterned carpet, predominantly the same pine-green as the walls. It smelled like breakfast. As he showed me to my red U-shaped booth, he pulled out the white cloth-covered table so that I could easily get into the bottom of the U-shaped seat. From that seat I could see the rest of the restaurant: the bar across from me, the red U-shaped booths like mine lining the east and west walls with a row of tables down the middle. Starched white tablecloths. Brass samovars on the ledges between each booth. *This is where I will take my fancy friends from now on,* I thought.

The rather loud smooth jazz seemed wrong for the scene. When you walk into an Italian restaurant and Frank Sinatra is singing "Come Fly with Me" or Rosemary Clooney is singing "Mambo Italiano" you know you are in an Italian restaurant. Even if it is a suburban strip mall pizzeria, you know they gave some thought about ambiance and want you to feel like you have entered their space. This is why I was surprised to hear that smooth jazz in the RTR, but it was soon replaced by more predictable 19th-century Romantic orchestral art music featuring a clarinet, a violin, or both. It was probably a greatest-hits collection of Russian composers.

The attentive waiters were dressed almost like 19th-century Russian soldiers, straight out of a Tolstoy novel, in dark double-breasted uniforms with gold buttons. My waiter, Sergei, brought me ice water and a tea menu. I chose the St. Petersburg Tea. As I awaited its delivery, I noticed the couple seated next to me. They were high-maintenance and late-middle-aged. They told Sergei their plans: the man's 94-year-old aunt would be joining them, so could they have a stand-alone chair in case Auntie couldn't navigate the booth seat? Then when Auntie arrived, they would ask her which seat she would prefer. They repeated this strategy to Sergei a number of times, and during these recitations inquired as to his name and place of origin. (That's how I learned he is Sergei from Gorky.) Additionally, they would be joined by two nieces around 1:30. It was now just a few minutes after 11:00, so they were camping out. (Is this what fancy people do?) They deferred their tea order until Auntie arrived.

I sat contentedly in my booth taking notes on the Auntie conversation until my little teapot was placed in front of me. It was accompanied by a teacup encased in metal, a small rectangular tray containing three little cups: one filled with white and brown sugar cubes, the second containing every kind of packaged sweetener imaginable, and the third cup held about a tablespoon of red berries. I wasn't sure what to do with the berries, so I quietly plopped about half of them in the cup with my tea. Next to the tray I found a small saucer with four tiny madeleine cookies. Aside from the pageantry of this grand course, I have to admit that the tea tasted ordinary to my unrefined palette. It sure looked fancy, though.

The long-awaited Auntie finally appeared amid much hubbub. Of course she did not create the hubbub, her nephew did. Even after the rehearsals, he seemed nervous asking her if she would prefer the booth seat or the stand-alone chair. "I'll just sit in the booth," she said, "after I let my driver know I'm okay." After a quick wave to the driver, she returned and nimbly slid into the booth. It was as if Auntie Mame had arrived. She went on to tell them about her fabulous driver and various mutual relatives with whom the couple seem to have lost contact.

Auntie didn't want tea. She wanted a concoction from the bar featuring vodka, orange juice, cranberry juice, and one other alcoholic ingredient I didn't hear. She told them about Cousin Dan as I ate my Kobe burger. Cousin Dan occasionally hits her up for money, and this last time, "I wrote him a check for $180,000 just to get rid of him."

As I ate my cheesecake adorned with cherries, the nephew began to speak. It seems he wrote a book which wasn't doing as well as he had hoped. Did Auntie think she could help him promote it? When he said his own name, I googled what I thought he said with various spellings just in case he was some famous author or celebrity I should know about. Nothing. Maybe he just wishes he were a famous author or celebrity. As I finished my dessert, I heard them say that they made their living in dry cleaning.

THE ROSE MUSEUM

With luscious cheesecake in my belly, I bid farewell to the colorful (in many ways) Russian Tea Room and wandered over to Carnegie Hall's Rose Museum in the Carnegie Hall Tower devoted to Carnegie Hall history. Behind glass I saw batons donated by famous conductors and programs autographed by Leonard Bernstein, Duke Ellington, and Yo-Yo Ma. The artifact that took my breath away was Benny Goodman's Buffet-brand clarinet. There, separated from me by a sheet of ordinary glass was the venerated instrument of my clarinet hero with which he played that historic 1939 Carnegie Hall jazz concert. This concert generated my favorite live recording of all time and which contains the hot-as-fire performance of "Sing, Sing, Sing." This concert was the first time jazz (specifically swing) was performed in that hall. After a tentative start (according to Goodman interviews), the players began to wail and the concert was a HUGE success! This was also the first time an integrated ensemble of any kind played on that stage. Benny Goodman always played in front of an integrated band assembled from the very best performers, and he wasn't about to change for Carnegie Hall. Beside his clarinet were Gene Krupa's drumsticks and Lionel Hampton's vibraphone mallets from that same concert. I walked around the exhibits, but came back to the clarinet. I bought some postcards in the little shop and then gawked at the clarinet some more. It looked just like my own Buffet-brand clarinet!

WINTERREISE

It was as if I put this dream concert together myself: the singer, the accompanist, the repertoire, the venue, and even the date were perfect. The singer, Ian Bostridge, wrote a book about the song cycle *Winterreise* which I happened upon in a bookstore a couple of years ago. I bought Bostridge's recording of the song cycle to compliment his book. One evening while sitting on the couch, I was thirsty for an interesting musical experience and wondered if he would be performing *Winterreise* anywhere soon. He would be, indeed, at Carnegie Hall where I'd always wanted to hear a concert, and as an extra bonus Thomas Adès would be playing the prominent piano part! Adès composed *The Tempest*, a 2004 opera very loosely based on Shakespeare's *Tempest*. It was so loosely based, that the man sitting next to me at a movie theater Metropolitan Opera Live in HD performance huffed, "This doesn't have anything to do with Shakespeare!" and walked out of the theater. He was not incorrect, but I was delighted by Adès's opera with Prospero (the rightful Duke of Milan), Ariel the spirit and her screeching aria and gymnastics performed on a chandelier, and the stormy maritime theme throughout. Adès charmed me in an interview presented during the Live in HD transmission, and now I would see him in-person playing the piano for *Winterreise* of all things, on a warm October day in Manhattan.

The concert day was finally here, and I found myself sitting in the most famous concert hall in the world wondering: who has been seated in this red-velveteen-upholstered chair for other concerts? Who sat here for Benny Goodman's in 1939? Who sat here when Gustav Mahler conducted the New York Philharmonic in 1910 (and what were they wearing)? Why didn't that person behind me unwrap their cough drop before the performance started? (Ricola supplies free cough drops at various locations in the "house.") The place actually seemed familiar because I had daydreamed about it so often since I bought my ticket.

FRANZ SCHUBERT

I dreaded purchasing the small study scores at the college bookstore when I learned that Romantic-era song cycles would be the subject of our graduate school Theory Seminar. I was not a fan of voice music, whether solo or in choirs. After some listening in the College of Music's Listening Library under the larger-than-life gaze of composers such as Paul Hindemith, Aaron Copland, Samuel Barber, and others, framed on the wall, I soon learned that Schubert songs (individuals or those in cycles) were pleasurable listening. The classic that everyone learns first is "Die Erlkönig," ("The Elfking"), the dramatic story of a boy and his father riding in a horse-drawn carriage through the woods. The point-of-view changes from son to father amid galloping hoofbeats represented with repeating low notes of the piano. The crisis is not exaggerated— the boy's soul is stolen by the Erlkönig.

Schubert composed songs and song cycles and the exemplar of the latter is *Winterreise*. These poems were written by German poet Wilhelm Müller as a monodrama. This means that the protagonist (the sad, weary traveler) plods through the cycle's 24 songs exploring his psyche with no other characters around. Schubert's setting of the poems into a song cycle is understood to be autobiographical, at least through metaphor, for himself or any singer who performs the cycle. For me as a listener, ever since the college Listening Library, this singer would be Dietrich Fisher-Dieskau, the music world's favorite Schubert interpreter. Fisher-Dieskau is gone now, and part of the reason I planned this music-nerd's Carnegie Hall excursion was to hear what other singers are doing with *Winterreise*. I own recordings of Ian Bostridge and Jonas Kaufmann performing the cycle, but I wanted to hear it live. Bostridge wrote that book about *Winterreise, Schubert's Winter Journey: Anatomy of an Obsession* in 2015. The book is small, thick, white-covered with the traveler's plodding footsteps embossed on the front, and the text printed on thick, glossy, fragrant, high-quality paper. While reading it, I get the feeling that I am examining Bostridge's psyche as well as Schubert's and Müller's.

Franz Schubert (1797-1828) was not part of fancy Viennese society. He did not attend balls and large concerts and operas. He was more likely to be found among a group of friends in someone's home salon or a coffee house sharing music and poetry and playing Charades. These gatherings came to be called Schubertiads to honor the innovative composer of art songs and chamber music meant for a small venue. (His large-scale works were not as remarkable.) He liked to take long walks in the country, sometimes with friends, because he found inspiration in nature. He was the king of unrequited love in his time, and in response made some unfortunate choices which resulted in his contracting syphilis in 1823. This diagnosis was a death sentence at that time, and might even be accompanied by dementia. Schubert died at his brother's house in 1828. The epitaph on his tombstone reads: "The art of music has buried here a rich possession, but still fairer hopes" (Franz Grillparzer, 1791-1872).

Many of the simple, everyday song titles in this cycle belie the depth of feeling expressed: "The Weather Vane," "The Linden Tree," "Dream of Spring," "Rest," "The Crow," and "The Organ Grinder." Add to this list titles like "Frozen Tears," "Numbness," and "The Stormy Morning." Consider that the weather vane is a traditional symbol of infidelity, the dream of spring represents lost youth and love lost forever, and the crow is a predator stalking the wanderer and the listener gets a sense of what she's in for.

The literary motif of the *Lindenbaum*, or linden tree, dates back to medieval Germany where it is usually associated with love or serves as a lovers' rendezvous spot. In his book, Ian Bostridge tells us that the linden tree is a "magical, mythical tree" and groves of linden trees are places of pilgrimages. The fifth song of *Winterreise* is "The Lindenbaum," composed with the simplicity and straightforwardness of major chords and scales. The art song has metamorphosed into a folk song in German and Austrian culture with only minor changes from the Schubert original. (Even Bart Simpson sang it!) The modified folk song version is often used in community singing situations where it is taken way out of context from the *Winterreise* original which starts out in glorious nature (a favorite Romantic-era theme) but twists into something dark and sinister. The branches of the linden tree attempt to lure the traveler to rest underneath. You know and he knows what would happen if he did. It is winter and he would freeze to death. Death is another favorite theme of the Romantics. Performed as an art song by itself or as a pseudo-folksong, "The Lindenbaum" is a crowd-pleaser, probably the most popular song in the cycle.

Back in Theory Seminar in 1980-something, I aced my interpretive essay on "The Crow," the fifteenth of 24 songs in *Winterreise*. (Professor Epstein did not hand out A's easily!) The secret to an A grade was to analyze the music and the poetry persuasively and then synthesize the two showing how the music and the words relate. (Earlier that semester I had turned in a solid analysis of the music of "Numbness" but neglected to tie it in with the words: B-. I hadn't had my vocal epiphany yet.) There, hand-written in blue-ink cursive on five-hole-punched filler paper before word processors changed the world, is a successful analysis of "The Crow!" Look how similar these green-inked cursive words I'm writing today are to those blue words of thirty-something years ago. Each letter was formed then exactly how I would form it now. But what did I say with those words back then? At approximately two-thirds of the way into the song (measure 29 to be exact) the music for the piano's left hand goes low into the bass clef as the music descends. The traveler has realized that the crow sees him as prey and beseeches the bird:

"O crow, let me at last see
Faithfulness unto death!"

(Translated by Richard Stokes
in the Carnegie Hall program)

These two lines spoke to Schubert. He repeated them in his song setting even though they were not repeated in Müller's poem. In the sheet music, the singer is instructed to sing the German word *Grabe* loudly. (The word is poetically translated either as 'ending' or 'death' but the German word means literally 'grave.') My analysis interprets the descending motion of the music as movement toward the grave for the Traveler, but also for the depressed composer who would be dead from syphilis within the year.

Schubert's music for this poem also features a repeating triplet motif (three notes to a beat instead of the usual two or four.) The triplets never stop until the very last chord of the song giving the sensation of perpetual motion. I've since learned that this is a common device of Schubert's (he used it in "Die Erlkönig" to represent the dramatic horse-hooves). Back then in my "A" paper, I identified the triplets as representing the movement of the crow. I was on-target as this evoked a rare red "Yes!" in the margin from Professor Epstein.

These are the kinds of musical features a Music Theory scholar would notice after careful study. But in the concert hall, the poems go by too fast to identify motifs and to try to translate the German. Many listeners notice these features subliminally, and others are already familiar with the cycle. Most listeners will notice the *Gestalt* of the cycle: the overall sense of desperation with faint glimmers of hope and brightness. The prominent piano part intertwined with the vocal lines is notable because the piano is usually in the background.

Ian Bostridge sang these songs as if he were having a conversation with the audience. His hand gestures and facial expressions seemed more suited for a small room of friends than a huge concert hall, in fact the most famous on the planet. This is how Schubert himself performed *Winterreise* when the cycle was new, for seventy uninterrupted minutes at a Schubertiad at his friend Franz von Schober's house in Vienna in front of a group of curious friends. They found the songs gloomy, but Schubert said, "I like these songs more than all the rest, and you will come to like them as well." Perhaps he liked these songs because they represented so well his mood knowing that, like the Wanderer in the songs, he would soon be lying in his grave.

The last song of the cycle is "Der Leiermann," or "The Hurdy-Gurdy Man." The words describe the man as cold and remote, bringing forth music without feeling. Susan Youens suggests in the program notes that this meaningless repetition is like a "living death." The music goes on and on with no possibility of transcendence expressed. Could this be Schubert's syphilitic dementia? Or could this be Schubert's imagining of syphilitic dementia?

I relished my music-nerdness during my Russian Tea Room/Carnegie Hall daytrip. It occurred to me that I could have enjoyed this same outing eighty years ago: the Russian Tea Room, Carnegie Hall, and Schubert's *Winterreise* are institutions that have been around at least that long. Could I ever plan another excursion as nerdly perfect as this one?

Portraits

The tall redhead wrapped a silk scarf around her neck as the rest of the group bumped up their cameras' ISO settings. Our instructions were to make the beach background look dark so that the lighting on the subject would make the portrait pop. This was part of a winter 2013 portrait photography workshop in Cape May organized by a local publishing company that caters to the interests of tourists, but at the same time actively contributes to the quality of life of year-round residents with events like this. The photography teacher was on their staff. We learned what lens to use for portraits (something with an 85-100mm range to eliminate the distortion a wide-angle lens will create), what aperture to use generally (f/11 to get sharpness and depth on the face), to have the camera at eye level and to shoot at the eyes. These are the standard rules, but once they are learned, the photographer will naturally experiment. For example, holding the camera above the subject's head will make them look like they are leaning in and camouflage extra chins. We learned about lighting and then shot portraits of each other in the dimly-lit studio, in a sunny room in a Victorian-era hotel, and in bright sunlight on the beach. We learned how to compose a portrait of a subject in front of a window which was at the same time reflecting the yellow hotel and its white columns.

I figured out when shooting my subjects that I got much better results when I attempted to chat them up. They'd answer a question and I'd get the shot of them looking relaxed, or I would try to surprise them with a weird comment. I like being behind the camera, but I also enjoy studying the masters and gleaning ideas from them. I never thought much about portraits, though. I usually shoot landscapes, flowers, and animals.

I looked at an old Smithsonian guide before a D.C. conference trip and saw a portrait of Henry David Thoreau which was supposed to be on display at the National Portrait Gallery. This was the treasure I wanted to search for because I'm still lost in admiration of Thoreau from last spring's Concord trip. Whenever I visit a new museum I like to identify an artifact or artwork to search out. I browse through museum websites, guidebooks, or library books for a piece that grabs my eye. It's like a treasure hunt. I searched low and high for Thoreau in the Gallery, from the first floor on Wednesday to the third floor on Sunday. I found other author portraits from the period (Nathaniel Hawthorne, Edgar Allan Poe) and other Transcendentalists (Margaret Fuller, Harriet Beecher Stowe), but no Henry David Thoreau. I was distracted from the Thoreau treasure hunt by a dizzying collection of historical portraits, an exhibit of Herman Leonard's black and white photographic portraits of jazz musicians, and another exhibit nearby of Carl Van Vechten's portraits of Harlem Renaissance artists, musicians, writers, and notables. I'd be delivering a lecture on the Harlem Renaissance the following week, and looked at this art with great interest. I could not, however, find that Thoreau.

I made a game out of looking for the various ways hands were posed as I wandered the National Portrait Gallery. Many of the portraits don't show hands at all, but portray subjects from the shoulders up as we did in the Cape May workshop. The portraits which did show hands showed them holding an object that identified the subject's career or interests, or sometimes pointing to an important object in the room. Presidents are often shown standing, with fingers of one hand touching their desk or chair.

Christopher Columbus, in a 1584 engraving, points at the stars. In a 1796 Gilbert Stuart oil painting, George Washington gestures toward the symbolic objects from his military and presidential career placed on a table. Harriet Tubman folds her hands in front of her in an 1885 photograph. Louisa May Alcott reads a paper she holds in front of her in an 1870 portrait, and in 1904, Helen Keller keeps her right hand on a Braille book while her left hand holds a rose to her nose. Lucille Ball (1944), Georgia O'Keefe (1956), and dancer Bill T. Jones (1985) pose their hands dramatically. In her 1933 portrait, Katharine Hepburn's hands are styled into an arabesque in front of her side-facing face. The Gallery displays her four Oscar awards near her portrait, and

I snuck a quick iPhone photo of those statuettes with her portrait behind them. I loved that juxtaposition. Louis Armstrong (1935) holds his trumpet with his right hand while holding his famous white hanky to his cheek with his left hand. In a colorful 2006 oil painting by Jennie Summerall, Pulitzer Prize winning entomologist E.O. Wilson holds a twig covered with red insects.

I spotted my favorite hand portrait near the end of my visit to the Gallery. Among the presidential portraits is a handsome Franklin D. Roosevelt oil painting from 1945 by Douglas Granvill Chandor. This was a study for a larger planned painting called *The Big Three at Yalta*. This large (43.5 by 35.5 inch) oil-on-canvas shows FDR posed behind a table wearing a suit with a teal-colored tie, and a satin-lined cape over his shoulders. His hands are crossed on the table, and his left hand holds a lit cigarette in one of those long, sophisticated holders. What's notable, and most interesting, is that the canvas beneath the president's portrait shows a pencil drawing of the completed portrait group. It would have also included Prime Minister Winston Churchill and Premier Joseph Stalin with FDR seated in the middle. Eight oil-painted Roosevelt hand choices, holding pencils, eyeglasses, and a cigarette without a holder are depicted next to the pencil-drawn group. One of the hands is writing "OK FDR" in red on the canvas. It is as if I could cut out the hand options and try them on FDR as if he were a big paper doll. Which hands would you like to wear today, Mr. President? It's a shame that The Big Three at Yalta was never painted, but this study is fascinating for its look into the artist's ruminations on the subject's hands.

I never located that elusive Thoreau portrait at the National Gallery: I had to give up and ask the man at the information desk. He checked the paper binder of all the art on display and did not find it. Then he walked over to the computer to check the database. (There's a database?!?! Yes, I could have checked it, too, on the National Portrait Gallery's website.) My Thoreau, a ninth-plate daguerreotype by Benjamin D. Maxham from 1856 (2 1/2 by 1 7/8 inches) is "not on view" at the moment. I was more relieved that I didn't miss the tiny portrait, because if I had walked by Henry David without paying my respects I would have felt awful. It turns out that the Smithsonian guidebook I had consulted before the D.C. trip was twenty years old. (How did that happen?) Thoreau's daguerreotype was on view then, but it's in storage now in order to preserve the fragile artifact.

I enjoyed the portrait-taking in Cape May, but was disappointed to find very few people willing to sit for a portrait afterwards. Essayist Sir Max Beerbohm contradicted me a hundred years ago: "It seems to be a law of nature that no man ever is loth to sit for his portrait." That's not what I experienced, Sir Beerbohm. With a lack of human subjects willing to sit for me, I turned to animal friends. Gladys the Shetland Sheepdog is always willing to sit for a portrait and has a most expressive face which includes one blue and one brown eye. When I feature the blue eye, she has a skeptical look for some reason. On the beach she seems to be saying, "Are you kidding? I am not going to get my fur wet." When I feature the brown eye, she seems to be lobbying for extra treats. She's employing those "puppy dog eyes." I have photos of just her paws which always make me smile. Animal portraits seemed to be a good way to practice portraiture. Off I went to the Cape May County Zoo where the portrait subjects are a captive audience—literally. What would the animals at the zoo do for my camera?

My best wild animal portrait from a recent visit to the zoo featured the Siberian tiger named Rocky. The shot shows him looking straight at the camera with his tongue involved in what looks like a smile. I prefer to interpret it as a smile and not him thinking of how tasty I would be for dinner. Those eyes of his are big and expressive, but there's no way of knowing if I'm interpreting the look correctly. Aside from the unfortunate but quite necessary chain-link fence between him and me, this portrait is near perfect.

A brown alpaca with a white face posed for a portrait looking right at me from his habitat below the elevated visitor boardwalk where I stood. Her eyes are warm and long-lashed, and her mouth is permanently smiling. This gal seems to be saying, "Oh hello, human. Thanks for stopping by. Did you bring carrots?"

"One of these days I'll have to show you where my will is and tell you the password to my safe," said the woman in the orange baseball cap to the young man next to her. Then she told him about a lecture she'd been to and Jazz @ Juilliard. As usual when I'm alone, my ears searched the room for an interesting conversation to eavesdrop. Being retired in New York City would not be a bad thing, I thought, but one would need considerable supplies of money to attend shows and events, and pay rent, too. Then their conversation turned to Picasso.

I daytripped to Manhattan to attend some events at the Metropolitan Museum of Art focused on the photographs of the late Diane Arbus. There was an exhibition of Arbus's photographs in the Met's Breuer Building, a slide show with narration in the Grace Rainey Auditorium of the main museum building (this is where I was eavesdropping), and finally a panel of Arbus experts and exhibit curators. It seemed like a nice way to spend a Saturday. The photographs in the Breuer exhibit were hung on flat columns, one framed photo on each side of the column with lots of space around them to circulate. One of the exhibit designers told us that he got the idea and proportions for these columns from the Acropolis in Athens. There were no photos hung on the four perimeter walls, and those were painted a deep midnight blue inspired by the Manhattan sky at dusk, according to a curator. It was an unusual but effective exhibit viewing experience. I like knowing these details about art and exhibits.

The Picasso conversation ended abruptly when the slide show started. Diane Arbus's narration was surprisingly flippant and totally extemporized. She seemed embarrassed to be speaking about her own work. She informed her audience that there are things nobody would see unless she photographed them, and I believe her. She has photographed circus performers out of the ring on their own time, regular people going about their day-to-day activities, and generally imperfect, unbeautiful people just how they are. She is shooting portraits. Every subject held an interesting item, wore a costume, or stood with props that identified them. Arbus giggled as she described her subjects and how she had to coax them to pose. She even giggled about the nude subjects.

I checked-out a library book on Diane Arbus's work to study her photographic style before attending the events of her day in Manhattan. Her portraits are distinctive, and even after this small amount of study I could identify her work. A friend of mine told me, "I really don't like Diane Arbus's work. It's always as if she's invading her subjects' privacy and profiting on their freakishness." Maybe he's right, but I find her portraits captivating. She's a person who learned the rules of portraiture but frequently adjusted them to suit her needs. I'm not going to lie: some of her photos make me feel a bit uncomfortable because of their intimacy in the sense that she was intruding in the subjects' private backstage worlds. On the other hand, I can make a case for the argument (Arbus's own) that she was documenting a culture that few viewers would ever see. In any case, the photos are compelling.

My favorite of her shots is the small boy with a toy hand grenade. She told us in her narration that this boy had been happy to pose for her, but she took so many shots trying to capture just what she wanted that he started making this pained expression. It's priceless. It's cute in a bratty kind of way. In my mind, that image characterizes the oeuvre of Diane Arbus.

The little boy's face is tense. Is that a faux-pugilistic look, related to the toy grenade in his hand? No, Diane Arbus tells us, it's just that he's frustrated with her. So the boy's facial expression has been inspired by the photographer, much like my Cape May workshop subjects were influenced by me. They didn't know where to put their eyes before I started talking to them. They didn't know where to look. I'm not a great small-talker, but I was able to fake it then just long enough to get them to look at the camera inquisitively or amusedly. Did the artists behind the photographs and paintings in the National Portrait Gallery influence their subjects' portraits, too?

The animal portraiture initiative was going well until I got to the kookaburra, the peacock, the goose, and the horned owl outside in the challenging bright sunlight. The birds are too hard to see. Inside the tropical bird building, I photographed the small white egret, many scarlet ibises, a roseate spoonbill, and the vibrant flamingo who sauntered over to me for a closer look. The birds are magnificent, but there's something missing. Birds' eyes are small, flat, black discs set into the sides of their heads. There is no indication that they see me or even hope that I brought dinner. The zoo mammals, even the carnivorous tiger, interact with the photographer on some level. The birds don't. There is no depth to their gaze, and no recognition. The tropical bird house was good plumage photography practice, but not portraiture preparation.

I consulted my bird books to find out about bird eyes, and found nothing. However, I did notice bird feet in those pages. The Kookaburra and the Great Horned Owl I saw in the zoo are perchers, so they have a lot of strength in their toes. The owl, being also a bird of prey, has foot power plus sharp talons for…preparing meals. Most birds have three toes facing forward and one facing backwards which helps when perching or with balance in the case of walkers. The egret, Roseate Spoonbill, Scarlet Ibis, and flamingo are walkers and waders, so they have four long, skinny toes including the one pointing backwards for balance. Those toes act as mini tripods (more accurately quadripods if that is a word) to help the birds stand comfortably. Bird feet are distinctive and can help the bird watcher make a positive ID: a Great Egret has black feet with a yellow beak while the Snowy Egret has bright yellow with a black beak.

Inspired by a lecture I'd recently heard which mentioned Auguste Rodin, the sculptor, advising Rainer Maria Rilke, the writer in Aesthetics, I visited the Rodin Museum in Philadelphia. After decades living in the area and countless trips up the famous Rocky steps to visit the Philadelphia Museum of Art, I had never stopped in at the Rodin just a stone's throw away. The big sculptures I associate with Rodin are outside in the garden: *The Thinker* and *The Shades*, but inside the small museum I learned that Rodin was fond of busts. There were busts of Honoré de Balzac, Victor Hugo, and Gustav Mahler, just like the one I saw in the Vienna Opera. Busts are a kind of portrait, aren't they? Indeed there were plenty on-display at the National Portrait Gallery, but these works by Rodin surprised me in the midst of my thinking about portraits. The description next to the Mahler bust explained that Mahler was freaked out by Rodin measuring his head in all directions in order to sculpt a proper bust. Painters don't measure for a portrait, do they? Mahler got over it in any case and the two became friends.

"Rodin believed everything is in the hands," I heard the docent say to her group. They were looking at a small sculpture called *Cathedral* of two hands coming up out of the base and forming a steeple shape. At first glance, it looks like both hands belong to the same person. On closer inspection, the looker realizes that they are both right hands. They belong to two different people, and while so close to each other they are not touching.

I thought I was being whimsical in the National Portrait Gallery looking to see how portrait subjects' hands are depicted. Rodin was way ahead of me, studying and depicting the hands alone. Besides *Cathedral* and its sensual, gentle hands, there's a clenched hand which conveys tension and stress.

There's also Rodin's own hand (in marble?), gingerly holding a tiny woman's torso. I was onto something with those expressive hands.

Examining the art of portraiture and practicing my own skills, I became acutely aware of subjects' hands. The hands lead the viewer to unexpected insight about the subject's personality or how they wish to be seen. I translate this into an important photography lesson, to be conscious of my subjects' hands (or paws). These are the most expressive parts of the person (or animal). I wish we could go back for a Part Two of that Cape May workshop where we could talk about the placement, lighting and expressiveness of our subjects' hands. Isn't it curious that we didn't even consider hands that day?

I have a story about hands which I will never forget. When my sister and I were taking a last look at our mother at her funeral, I was conscious of my own typical, grief-ridden denial. Her face didn't look like her own face in spite of the undertaker's best efforts. Was this really her? Really? People were waiting on us and I was going to have to tear myself away from her forever, but I wasn't satisfied. In that moment, I remembered her hands! I was recalling how, recently, when I looked at my own hands I saw hers. I wear no rings, and in her later years, my mother didn't, either.

Her fingernails were the same shape as mine. Recently, my hands had started to show the freckles and age spots I always remembered on hers. I averted my gaze from her face to her familiar hands. Yes, I thought, this is my mother, and just like that my denial period ended, and I could slowly walk away from the coffin.

My last look at my mom, my mental portrait, was not her face but her hands. Her familiar hands.

Margaret Montet

"Jeanne, Are We Norma Desmond?"

Featured in more than one old movie and my mother's 1940s scrapbook, Angels Flight is a relic of another time in Los Angeles.

My old red scrapbook of autographed movie star photos is not in my closet, or in the cabinet with my college notebooks, or in the bookcase with my new scrapbooks. I was thinking of it as Fred, my boyfriend, or, boyFred, and I rode the NJ Transit train to Manhattan. We had reservations for the Turner Classic Movies (TCM) Classic Movie Locations Tour which would take us around the city to visit famous sites we had seen in old movies. Fred wasn't as fond of old movies as I was, so I was hoping the tour would be interesting to him. He would have been amused by the old red scrapbook. New-movie-watching is, to me, like appreciating art, but old-movie-watching is time travel. In his 1961 novel, *The Moviegoer*, American writer Walker Percy sums up the film-going experience: "The fact is I am quite happy in a movie, even a bad movie. Other people, so I have read, treasure memorable moments in their lives."

Watching the original 1977 *Star Wars*, I'm a frizzy-haired young teenager who stood in line with her parents one summer day to see that new blockbuster. Dad and I were both exhilarated by it, but Mom didn't like it so much. Watching *The Sound of Music* from 1965, I'm a carefree child with Shirley-Temple sausage curls identifying with the youngest von Trapp, Gretel. *Out of Africa* transports me to 1985, the mullet years, and the last big movie palace in Philadelphia where I watched that film with my best college friend. Movies, just like photographs, capture a moment in time. They record how the actors looked at the time they were made, they capture the director's vision, and they capture moments in a viewer's life. (Where did you see *Ghostbusters? Titanic? Forrest Gump? Brokeback Mountain?*) My favorite movies have stayed with me as I've aged. These days, I keep my hair short and I'm more likely to watch a movie on television. When I saw TCM's (Turner Classic Movies, my default channel) advertisement for their New York City Classic Movie Locations Tour on TV, I signed us up.

As we rode through ten railroad commuter stops (Princeton, New Brunswick, Newark, etc.) in Central-Northern New Jersey, I thought about the origins of that red scrapbook. Back in college, Jeanne showed me how she wrote to her favorite movie stars to request autographed pictures. "Could I please use the newest edition of *Who's Who in America?*" This book was kept behind the university library's reference desk because the librarians used it often to answer reference questions. We took the book to a table and Jeanne would write down the name and address of each star's management agency in her notebook. Later on, she wrote a brief letter to the star, in care of their management, and sent it away via snail mail. Back then, snail mail was the only mail. Jeanne had an impressive collection of these autographed photos which we chose to believe were signed by the stars themselves. We agreed that there was a good chance some assistant signed them. I was inspired by Jeanne's collection and started my own. I wrote to some of her stars because I thought they were a safe bet (Bette Davis! Jimmy Stewart!), and I looked up some of my own favorites. Jeanne has her star photos hung along her stairway now, and I'm supposed to have that red scrapbook. Where was it, though?

Well, I'd think about that later. Our train was pulling into New York's Penn Station where we would "detrain" and climb a few flights of stairs to 7th Avenue. I always turn right at 34th Street on my way to the theater district so that I can look at Macy's decorated windows. This day, for the first time ever, I noticed an old brass plaque from 1938 on Macy's façade. It's funny that I should notice it this day, as we were headed to the TCM tour, because it commemorates the place, formerly Koster & Bial's Theater, where Thomas Edison projected the first motion picture to a paying audience in 1896. This would coincidentally be a trivia question on the bus, and I looked smart for knowing the year.

THE SIGNIFICANCE OF MOVIES

I listed my favorite movies recently, those that I watch when I have a frustrating day or just need a boost. I call them my Go-To movies, and I was surprised to notice that they all have prominent music. If music isn't part of the story, there is a notable soundtrack: consider *The Sound of Music*, *Mary Poppins* (1964), *When Harry Met Sally* (1989), *Bridget Jones' Diary* (2001), and *Out of Africa*. These Go-To movies are in my permanent DVD collection and transport me to another time or place, or just create a happy mood.

My friends Brian and Jill have a list of Go-To movies with which they identify as a couple. After their children go to bed, they often relax with a viewing of *The Great Gatsby* (1974), *The Sting* (1973), *Jane Eyre* (1944), or *Breakfast at Tiffany's* (1961). I get the sense that they are not so much reminiscing as checking in on friends Daisy Buchanan, Henry Gondorff, Johnny Hooker, Holly Golightly. Watching my Go-To movies I feel like I'm visiting with Mary Poppins, Gretel von Trapp, Karen Blixen, and Sally Albright. Are they still the same? If Karen Blixen is managing her coffee plantation in Africa, and Sally Albright is walking around in Central Park, and Mary Poppins is dancing with Dick van Dyke and a bunch of animated penguins, then the world is in balance. I had hoped to see some locations from *When Harry Met Sally*, the only film on my Go-To list set in Manhattan. We did: the spot where they bought the Christmas tree in the Upper West Side.

When I saw my college friend Jeanne recently, I asked her if she had a list of Go-To movies. She knew exactly what I meant without further explanation: "*Charade* (1963), *Rear Window* (1954), *To Catch A Thief* (1955), *High Society* (1956), *North by Northwest* (1959), *The Sting!*" I know she had already thought about her favorites because she had her analysis ready. "I like romance stories mixed with thriller and mystery plots, but I tend to look for my favorite stars, too." Jeanne also confessed a predilection for black and white movies (even though her Go-Tos are in color) because she appreciates the technical stuff (lighting for example) and the suggestion of color when there are none.

BoyFred and I walked north on Broadway in the freezing Manhattan January cold to our tour meeting place, and I recalled images from this place with my parents since toddlerhood. Mom was comfortable with urban life because she used to come to Manhattan with her sisters. She told me so many stories about their adventures on Broadway and watching movies at Radio City Music Hall that her fondness for the city passed to me. When she was in the earlier stages of dementia, I could use the magic of VHS and DVD (which she never understood) to make a favorite movie appear on the television screen. There would be recognition and enjoyment and the frustration and anxiety of a faulty memory would be mollified, if only temporarily. We would usually watch musicals: *The Sound of Music, The King and I* (1956), and *Oliver!* (1968) or classics like *Little Women* (with Katharine Hepburn or June Allyson playing Jo from 1933 or 1949, because the newer one from 1994 with Wynona Ryder would have just confused her).

A few decades ago, my father and I would watch war movies. He seemed to be more content after his debilitating stroke if I were simply present in the room while he viewed his movies. I was happy to be there especially since my presence seemed to calm him. Even as a teenager I enjoyed quiet hobbies like embroidery and quilting which could be done in that situation. We didn't discuss the movies because he couldn't. Aphasia took his power of conversation away. Aphasia, or the inability to speak the words you're thinking, was a result of the stroke he had when he was 65, during my senior year of high school. Through hard work he had gained back some of his speech, but even at his best he was hard to understand. It was more frustrating for him than it was for me, I suspect. Now and then something in a movie would spark a U.S.

Coast Guard World War II memory and he would try to tell me. I know we watched William Holden and Alec Guinness in *The Bridge on the River Kwai* (1957), *The Halls of Montezuma* (1950) with Richard Widmark, and William Holden again in *Stalag 17* (1953). I know we didn't watch *From Here to Eternity* (1953). That one had too much mushy stuff for Dad, but has become a favorite of mine. Sitting in that sunny living room with Dad, I felt like we were forging a connection that had nothing to with war movies. For him, it was important just to have someone in the room even if traditional communication was difficult.

Before I knew I would be writing about age and movies, my friend Joe and I had a conversation about movies he uses in class. He's a lover of old movies, too, and watched many favorites with his mother. He teaches English Composition, in which students learn about drama, poetry, and fiction, and ultimately produce a ten-page literary research paper. We librarians help with that last task. Sometimes metaphor and symbolism are lost on me: the significance of the watermelon on the picnic table, the placement of the accent rug in the rumpus room, or the character's frustration with a stuck bedroom window. I wondered why Joe used Frank Capra's *Arsenic and Old Lace* (1944) in his course. Was it simply just a charming movie version of a play about two elderly slapstick serial killers or was there something deeper I didn't see? Joe explained that he uses the movie to show farce, black humor, and comedy mixed with drama. "There's a book upstairs in the library by Mark Fearnow which discusses how while World War II was brewing in Europe people in the United States wanted to resume their normal domestic lives now that the Great Depression was over. I think the book is called *The American Stage and the Great Depression.*[*] The older aunts in Arsenic are stuck in a past age and Mortimer is trying to make the killing stop." Joe often speaks like this, fully citing books he's read and summarizing their importance to our conversation.

I promptly fetched the book from the stacks after our conversation and read the section about *Arsenic and Old Lace.* The character, Mortimer, Fearnow suggests, represents the audience, incredulous at the prospect of two old ladies murdering men and burying them in the basement with the help of their nephew, Mortimer's evil brother Jonathan. (Mortimer is portrayed by Cary Grant in the movie.) The original play was written by Joseph Kesselring in 1941 as Hitler was coming into power in Europe and just before the Japanese bombed Pearl Harbor. Americans were afraid of Hitler and murder, and this lighthearted treatment of homicide gave them some release. The audience was comforted when Mortimer triumphed over Jonathan. Mortimer is afraid he will turn into Jonathan just as Americans were afraid they'd be forced to "turn into" Germany. The aunts represent American isolationists according to Fearnow, naïve and sentimental. Mortimer must triumph over them, too. I never would have read all that into the quirky little movie my friend shows in his class, but I'm comforted by the analysis because it

---

[*] Fearnow, Mark. *American Stage and the Great Depression: A Cultural History of the Grotesque* (Cambridge Studies in American Theatre and Drama). Cambridge University Press, 1997.

assigns gravitas to this superficially lighthearted film.

Back in Manhattan, Fred and I continued north on Broadway, finally arriving at our meeting location, Ellen's Stardust Diner, in the heart of the Theater District. This is the place where the servers spontaneously break out in song while diners enjoy their meal. Unfortunately, we didn't have time for breakfast because we were concerned about finding our tour guide. The reservation acknowledgment advised us to look for someone carrying a red TCM umbrella. I didn't see faces: most people I encountered had scarves wrapped around their noses and mouths. No one was outside unless they had to be. In spite of that, I met Lucy, a film major from California. She was waiting for the TCM tour, too, and we had a nice chat while scanning for the TCM umbrella. Lucy recommended TCM's Los Angeles tour to me since I had plans to go there in the spring. "I LOVED it," she said. "The bus takes you by the Muppets' studio and you'll see a statue of Kermit the Frog there on top of the gate. He's dressed like Charlie Chaplin because that used to be his studio!"

NEW YORK TOUR

Finally we found Sarah, an actress wrapped up in a quilted coat appropriate for an Arctic expedition and holding the TCM umbrella. An unmarked bus drove up and Sarah herded us onto it. *This isn't the big red bus in the commercial*, I thought. Sarah read my mind and explained that the big red bus with the giant TV screen was having mechanical issues. Instead, we had tiny screens throughout the bus. These were okay, but I'd see in April how much better the big screen is. Paul our driver worked that bus through the cramped streets and found places to pull over so that we could get out and explore. As we began our journey scenes from *On the Town* (1949) appeared on the little screens. This set a 1940s mood. This movie filmed a few scenes in New York (at the Empire State Building, Brooklyn Navy Yard, and Brooklyn Bridge), but the rest was shot on a Hollywood soundstage.

We would not be staying in the 1940s. TCM television host Robert Osborne popped up on our screen to introduce himself, welcome us on the tour, and explain that TCM doesn't have an iron-clad rule about what makes a "classic" movie. He explained that movie viewers have their own definitions of what is classic. (In other words, movies from the 1980s and 1990s would be included on this tour.) It felt like a disclaimer in case anyone complained that something was left out or an unexpected newer film was included. Then Robert Osborne invited us to notice "how much and how little" New York has changed. Comparing then and now, movie clip and reality would be an engaging exercise for Fred or anyone else who hasn't seen most of the movies.

Robert Osborne finished his welcome speech and we turned our attention back to Sarah. As we entered the Upper West Side, her banter accelerated. Almost every building has a story about movies being filmed there or movie stars living there. The Dakota at 1 West 72nd Street has both: I knew it as the apartment building where John Lennon was fatally shot, but creepy *Rosemary's Baby* (1968) was filmed there, too. Sarah said it was New York's first luxury apartment building when it opened in 1884, and both Leonard Bernstein and Judy Garland have lived there.

Actress Maureen O'Sullivan owned an apartment in the nearby Langham Building (135 Central Park West) and gave it to her daughter Mia Farrow. That apartment, along with Farrow, appeared in Woody Allen's *Hannah and her Sisters* from 1986. We saw a clip from *You've Got Mail* (1998) where the Meg Ryan character accidentally gets in the cash-only line at the Upper West Side's Zabar food store intending to pay with a credit card. The Tom Hanks character comes to her rescue. We disembarked at Zabar's to check out the location also familiar from a Woody Allen film, *Manhattan* (1979). We got snacks at Zabar's: I bought a strawberry cheesecake candy bar and Fred opted for a plastic container of snap peas. Also on the Upper West Side, the Irish bar in *The Apartment* (1960) is now a Kate Spade store, and Meg Ryan's bookstore from *You've Got Mail* is now an organic dry cleaner.

As we crossed Central Park on our way to the Upper East Side, I was compiling a list of New York movies to watch and reacquaint myself with: *Barefoot in the Park* (1967), *On the Town* (1949), *It Should Happen to You* (1954), Jeanne's Go-To *North by Northwest* (1959), and *Spellbound* (1945) all feature New York locations. One of my newer favorites has some crucial locations on the East Side. I never warmed up to Brian and Jill's Go-To *Breakfast at Tiffany's* until recently, but I've watched it a few times in recent years. I was especially excited to see the brownstone at 169 East 71st Street which was the façade of Holly Golightly's home in the movie. We got off the bus to walk down East 71st Street to the famous façade, pose for pictures in front of it, and get a feel for the neighborhood. The new owners bought it for over 90 million dollars and they are ripping out the insides. That's okay—the movie's interiors were shot on Hollywood soundstages anyway. Back on the bus, I won a TCM T-shirt for knowing the name of the cat in *Breakfast at Tiffany's*. ("Cat.")

We stopped also in the Sutton Place/Riverview Park neighborhood to see the 59th Street Bridge which has a prominent part in Woody Allen's *Manhattan* and in *My Man Godfrey* (1936). It's a chic neighborhood where, according to Sarah, Marilyn Monroe, Joan Crawford, Greta Garbo, and Humphrey Bogart lived. Before the fancy homes were here, there were run-down tenements. I'm not sure I want to know how that transition happened.

The New York tour ended at Grand Central Terminal, the famous railroad hub at 42nd Street and Park Avenue. Under the mesmerizing blue ceiling with glittering gold stars, scenes from *Spellbound* (1945), *The Thin Man Goes Home* (1945), *Jeanne's North by Northwest* (1959), and *Superman* (1978) were filmed. In another few months, I'd find myself at Union Station in Los Angeles, twice, at the ends of two L.A. sightseeing tours. (Is this a metaphor for moving on?) Fred and I finished our day with a casual dinner in the Hell's Kitchen section of Manhattan and then rode the NJ Transit train south to home, exhausted.

LOS ANGELES TOUR

During the following April, I was in Los Angeles for a conference and made time for some L.A. exploration. Earlier that week, my colleagues Mary and Kathy wanted to see the glamorous side of L.A., so we took a tour which began with the Hollywood Walk of Fame, the parts of Hollywood Boulevard and Vine Street sidewalks with two-foot pink stars embedded in gray terrazzo. Each features the name of an entertainer: actors, musicians, directors, and even fictional characters are celebrated here. This tour also took us to Beverly Hills, Santa Monica Pier, Olvera Street, Muscle Beach, and Venice Beach where we put our feet in the Pacific Ocean. We cruised down Sunset Blvd past the Whiskey-A-Go-Go. We covered a lot of ground, but out of all that, my favorite location was TCL's Chinese Theater (formerly Grauman's) where we found the foot- and handprints of the stars in the concrete. The stars of *Giant* (1956), *West Side Story* (1961), *The King and I* (1956), and *Star Trek* (1979) are co-located. Older stars from the 1930s and 1940s are in the center of the plaza. I snapped many photos of this kitschy Americana, and chose Humphrey Bogart's concrete square to post on Facebook: "SiD MAY YOU NEVER DiE TiLL i KiLL YOU—Humphrey Bogart. Aug. 21, 46." My first-grade teacher would have been horrified because he mixed lower-case 'i's with capital letters. That is a no-no. Clark Gable wrote a brief tribute to Sid in the concrete: "For Sid who is a great guy."

"Sid" is Sid Grauman (1879-1950) who created

many themed cinemas in California starting with Grauman's Egyptian Theater in 1922. The Chinese was his last theater. Grauman and co-owners Mary Pickford, Douglas Fairbanks, and Howard Schenk brought in Chinese artists and architects to create authentic features on the interior and exterior of the building. This theater opened in 1927, and its first big premiere that year was Cecil B. DeMille's *The King of Kings*. There are several legends about how the famous footprints in concrete got started. It might have been Norma Talmadge, Mary Pickford, or Sid Grauman himself who accidentally stepped in the concrete. Another story claims that the construction foreman, Jean Klossner, autographed his work in the concrete and inspired the movie star idea when Grauman saw the signature. Over the years since Grauman's death, the property has been owned by other parties. A Chinese company called TCL now owns the theater, making it officially TCL Chinese Theater, but most people still call it Grauman's in honor of Sid.

The highlight of my time in California and my last act of tourism there was the TCM Movie Locations Tour recommended by Lucy in front of Ellen's Stardust Diner in Manhattan. The big bus picked me up at my hotel, and with eager anticipation I climbed aboard as if I were Dorothy entering the Land of Oz. This tour felt different from the Manhattan tour immediately because the bus was equipped with an enormous television screen for viewing movie clips. The sides and part of the top of the bus were glass, and the rows of seats were stadium-style so that everyone had unobstructed sight lines. Looking through my movie-star shades on a sunny April day with an apple-berry smoothie in my belly, I was about to embark upon a Los Angeles-style adventure with thirteen other anonymous movie lovers, our live tour guide, and TCM host Ben Mankiewicz on the bus's giant movie screen. The sunshine, glitz, and glamour contrasted with the grit and freezing cold of New York City.

We drove past Hollywood High School where countless movie scenes were filmed and then past Jim Henson's Muppet Studios. There was the statue of Kermit the Frog posed like Charlie Chaplin on top of the fence just as Lucy in New York had described. Nearby is Ren Mar Studios where my favorite 1960s television shows *The Andy Griffith Show*, *That Girl*, *The Dick Van Dyke Show*, and many others were filmed. I hadn't even been thinking about TV shows, so this was a bonus. Ren Mar was at one time Lucy and Desi's Desilu Studios! (My notes from this part of the tour are hardly legible because I couldn't write fast enough.) There were the Ravenswood Apartments where Mae West lived. Wow: we saw the site of Ambassador Hotel where the wildly popular Cocoanut Grove Night Club used to be, the Brown Derby Restaurant, and Bullocks Wilshire Department Store where Jessica Fletcher worked.

Wait, no. I can never remember that actress's name because she's made such an impression on me as her late-in-life character, Jessica Fletcher on *Murder, She Wrote* which ran from 1984-96. That's the name I recall when she pops up on TCM in a movie—maybe *Gaslight* from 1944 or possibly *The Harvey Girls* from 1946. "Jessica—no. Jessica Fletcher—no. It begins with an 'A'…Anne…Alice…Abigail…Angela… Angela What?…" Once upon a time my parents tried to convince me that *Murder, She Wrote* was a great program, but when they were still around it seemed like an old person's show. Something happened, though: one summer when I had Lyme Disease. *Murder, She Wrote* marathons were on television and I *only* felt like watching TV. Crocheting felt too athletic to me that summer. The beach was out of the question. I became a believer in the mystery writer from Cabot Cove, Maine, and made the transition to a world where murders happened wherever this woman went. I admired her lifestyle, her circle of friends, her wardrobe and her clever scarf-tying. Now it is me who is aging and I'm finding peace in episodes of *Murder, She Wrote* and becoming a fan of her many old movies. It's Angela Lansbury, of course; it was Angela Lansbury who worked at Bullocks Wilshire Department Store *right there in front of me.*

On the other hand, Norma Desmond gives me the creeps. You know who that is, don't you—she's the main character in Billy Wilder's 1950 film, *Sunset Boulevard*, played by Gloria Swanson. Norma, as an aging, has-been movie star, utters the famous line, "Alright, Mr DeMille, I'm ready for my close-up." Besides the general creepiness I mentioned, she's delusional and thinks that she has another chance of stardom in DeMille's movie. What her close-up would reveal is a couple of grotesque, drawn-on, arched eyebrows perched atop wide-open eyes and heavy make-up. Is this look the result of a primitive facelift? Is that sneer Gloria Swanson's or Norma Desmond's?

I re-watched this movie recently, after I cruised down the actual Sunset Boulevard on that big, glassy tour bus. I was amused to see that the Paramount Studios façade portrayed in the film looks remarkably like Paramount Studios today. During this recent viewing of the film, I was horrified to learn that this washed-up, delusional star character has been assigned the age of fifty! That's not old. Her relationship with boytoy William Holden is uncomfortably odd. She gives him a gold cigarette lighter inscribed thus: "Mad about the Boy—Norma Desmond." Boy?

Eleven years after Sunset Boulevard, José Quintero's *The Roman Spring of Mrs. Stone* was released.* In this movie, Karen Stone, another aging character, is *approaching* fifty. Her much older husband died on a plane to Rome, and Mrs. Stone, portrayed by Vivien Leigh (Scarlett O'Hara) stays there without him. Her friend the Contessa, played by Lotte Lenya, introduces Mrs. Stone to much younger Paolo diLeo played by a boyish Warren Beatty. (Psssst…He's a gigolo, and I'll point out that while she buys him expensive gifts, she rarely gives him cash. Mrs. Stone is convinced that this takes away some of the scandal of their affair.) It's not the large age-difference that makes her just as disturbing as Ms. Desmond to me, it's the delusion and the desperate craving for male attention.

MacArthur Park is a real place. You may have heard the weird Jimmy Webb song recorded by a surprising array of singers including Richard Harris, Glen Campbell, Waylon Jennings, and Donna Summer.

*This story was adapted from a novella by Tennessee Williams.

We passed the park on the big TCM bus, across from the famous Park Plaza Hotel. I had the sensation that I'd seen these places before, but I'm not familiar with *The Hidden* (1987), *Volcano* (1997), *Kiss Kiss Bang Bang* (2005), or *Drive* (2011) which contain scenes from the park, or *Gangster Squad's* hotel scene from 2013. We stopped by the 1893 Bradbury Building built by a gold-mining millionaire to view its ornate wrought iron. Many movies including *The White Cliffs of Dover* (1944) and *The Artist* (2011) filmed some scenes here. Marvel Comics currently occupies offices in the Bradbury and sets some of their characters there. Nearby is another Grauman cinema, the Million Dollar Theater, which was showing *Pretty in Pink* when I was there, a favorite Andrew McCarthy (and Molly Ringwald) movie from 1986.

Near the Million Dollar Theater I recognized "Angels Flight" from my mother's 1940s scrapbook. It's the shortest funicular in the world, I learned, now closed because it is dangerous and passengers have died. It is seen in many films noir because of the unique way boarding houses were accessed from its steps. It gives a unique, gritty, urban feel to movie scenes.

It was peculiar that both of my Los Angeles tours ended up at Union Station. I was happy to see it twice because it has so much movie history. *Gone with the Wind*, *Stagecoach*, and *Goodbye, Mr. Chips* all from 1939 when the station was new, and even a movie called *Union Station* from 1950, had scenes filmed there. One huge room was transformed into a bank for Leonardo DiCaprio's 2002 *Catch Me If You Can*. I walked around gazing at the massive station, built in

1939 to consolidate a few passenger railroads in L.A. I was hungry, so I watched where our tour guide went for a snack: Wetzel's Pretzels. I walked on the ornate terracotta and marble floors under ridiculously high ceilings eating my yummy pretzel and then I spotted the old, closed-up Harvey House restaurant. Just like in the movie, *The Harvey Girls* (from 1946 and starring Judy Garland and Angela Lansbury among others), this restaurant was strategically placed for optimal walk-in traffic at the train station and once upon a time staffed by young ladies in puffy-sleeved uniforms who looked like Judy Garland and Cyd Charisse. The movie *The Harvey Girls* dramatized their story but Jessica… Angela Lansbury is in it, too, portraying a tough saloon singer in sequins. The railroad depicted in that movie's Oscar-winning song, "The Atchison, Topeka, and the Santa Fe" (Harry Warren and Johnny Mercer) actually did roll into this station.

The much-anticipated tour was all but over, and I walked back to the bus which would take me back to Hollywood. I became aware of a kind of soundtrack to my Union Station walkabout experience and near the bus discovered the music was coming from an enormous set of South American panpipes played by a man standing in a square at Olvera Street, the oldest part of Los Angeles across from Union Station. The music almost sounded like organ music, owing to the size and diameters of the pipes. Both kinds of pipes are cylindrical, and would create similar sound waves. They are fined-tuned by putting pebbles and dry corn into the bottoms of the pipes. Whenever I catch a glimpse of Union Station in a movie I'm going to think of those panpipes.

What did I learn from my focus on films? Movies, just like photographs, capture a moment. Movies record how the actors look, the director's vision, and the concerns of contemporary culture. If a movie was made years earlier or later, the people and places would look different and movie technology would be obviously more or less advanced. Characters in a 1930s movie based on a Jane Austen book look like 1930s people more than nineteenth century people, don't they? People age, even movie stars do. Movies made during war time betray an ambient anxiety as in *Arsenic and Old Lace*.

When I signed up for these movie tours in Manhattan and Los Angeles, I was simply hoping to enhance my understanding and appreciation for this art form through some fun sightseeing. As I read about movies and watched films like *Sunset Boulevard* and *The Roman Spring of Mrs. Stone* I was nagged by the dismal concept of age. Film depictions of women of a certain age have evolved since the 1940s and 1950s. It's not so bleak anymore--older characters are living active, happy, fulfilling lives. (I just watched Sally Field's 2015 film, *Hello My Name is Doris*.) "We've come a long way, baby," the Virginia Slims cigarette ad used to say. In this century we celebrate our older actresses: Meryl Streep, Judi Dench, Maggie Smith, Helen Mirren, and Sally Field. We admire the characters they play who tend to be independent thinkers rather than delusional caricatures. Maybe I'm incapable of impartiality about the following, but fifty no longer seems old. Classic movies have supplied for us a lesson about our culture.

Aging isn't so bad, I tell myself. *There's the evidence.* I still haven't located my red movie star scrapbook though.

Souvenirs of Barcelona

I neglected to research Montserrat before my group embarked upon this excursion. This two-dimensional tile rendering is the closest I got to the wildly popular medieval Black Madonna sculpture.

BARRIO GÓTICA: THE COLOR-BLOCK BAG

Our Barcelona hotel was situated in the center of Carrer de l'Argenteria, a narrow street which would allow one car to pass through at a time. On Saturdays and Sundays, vendors set up white tents where they'd sell handbags, scarves, and jewelry. On the first of fourteen days in that city, I saw those smart color-block, felted wool handbags and knew I'd purchase one soon. On my eighth day there, I bought one, multicolored with purple handles, and the vendor took me down a narrow medieval alley called Carrer de Manresa to his shop and factory so that I could pay with my credit card.

By this time, I was comfortable with these narrow passages because I realized they weren't alleys at all, but narrow streets leftover from the Middle Ages. The Museo Picasso de Barcelona is on Carrer de Montcada which is connected to the tiny street-labyrinth that brought me to my hotel. Carrer de Grunyi was the street under my room's skinny terrace. In Catalan, *carrer* means "street," *carrero* translates to "alley," and *via* means "way." The noisy, four-lane, road we walked along to get to our classrooms was Via Laietana. By the second week in Barcelona I much preferred those tiny carrers to the busy vias and I got the hang of navigating them.

Carrer de l'Argenteria, the hotel street where I bought the handbag, leads in one direction to the busy Via Laietana, and in the opposite direction terminates at the foot of the Basilica Santa Maria del Mar. A small group of us discovered this huge gothic basilica on our first day. Amy, Mark, Pearl and I, writing students in Barcelona for two weeks, wandered straight into a lively sunlit square at the foot of the old front steps of the basilica. We ordered lunch at a café there and I gawked at the basilica from under a sheltering umbrella as I waited for my *Tagliatelle Marinara*. Pearl was finished with her *Patatas Bravas*, a typical Catalan potato dish consisting of potato chunks under a spicy sauce, before Amy got her *Vegetarian Paella*.

When my Tagliatella Marinara finally arrived, I stared at it in disbelief. I was expecting a pasta with red sauce (marinara as we know it in the U.S.) but what sat in front of me was a bowl of naked spaghetti with mussels, clams, and other sea creatures to which I am allergic. Even eating that spaghetti around the creatures would have put me down for a few days. The server scolded me for not asking about the ingredients of the dish and I protested that where I came from, *marinara* meant a red sauce with no crustaceans. She schooled me: "Marinara means from the sea. *Mar* is the word for the sea." I understand the taxonomy, but that doesn't change the fact that where I live and any place I've been up to now, *marinara* has come to mean red meatless sauce. The server had little sympathy for me and I was left to mooch some of Amy's vegetable paella. We'd walk through that square in-between the basilica and the "marinara café" many times over the following two weeks in order to get to the El Born neighborhood and Amy's favorite vegetarian restaurant. No crustaceans adorned the food there, and I developed a fondness for the *Quarto Queso Pizza*. Although my tastes are far from vegetarianism, I was grateful for that restaurant because its food was safe from shellfish.

EL BORN: THE BOOK

From the vegetarian place around the corner from the "marinara café," I could see the side of Santa Maria del Mar. It's not an ostentatious church, but it has a comforting, protecting vibe to it. *Mar* means 'sea,' you'll remember, and this is the basilica of the men and women of the Middle Ages who made their living from the sea. There are ships and sea motifs throughout the church, mixed with the more typical Catholic statues and iconography. Our writing group toured the basilica and found out that it was built in collaboration between the working-class townspeople, the builders, and the famed architect and master builder Berenguer de Montagut. Two plaques on the front doors show men carrying large stone blocks strapped to their backs. The men are bent over from the weight of the blocks spread over the whole of their backs.

This is what actually happened: men from the El Born barrio (neighborhood) hiked up to the stone quarry on Möntjuic, Barcelona's own mountain on the other side of the city, and brought back stones for the cathedral builders. The builders planted tributes to the workers in the basilica. Although there is an ornate medieval cathedral nearby in El Barrio Gótica (the Gothic or medieval neighborhood), this is where the workers, tradesmen, fishermen, and other laborers worshipped. We were advised by our tour guide to get our hands on the bestselling historical novel, *Cathedral of the Sea* by Idelfonso Falcones, to learn more. I was lucky to find an English translation right there in the El Born area. I dove into its 751 pages a few months later, back in my American reality.

The main character of the book is Arnau Estanyol who was born outside of Barcelona, but became a resident of the city as a young child. He and his friend Joan (that's a guy) ran around Barcelona, exploring the city, meeting people, and describing some of the city's features that still exist today. At one point they hid in the as-yet unfinished Santa Maria del Mar and find their way underneath where they find a spooky Roman graveyard. (Is that fictional?) It's entertaining to read of Arnau's childhood adventures and mischief which take him to Santa Maria del Mar, the Born and Ribera neighborhoods, Möntjuic mountain, the beach, and the section we now call El Barrio Gótica. This is where the fancier, more ornate cathedral is.

Arnau missed the mother he never knew, and his father suggested that he think of the Blessed Mother Mary as his new mother. Through his childlike consciousness, he looked to the statue of her in Santa Maria del Mar as the representation of his mother figure. This powerful symbol stayed with him throughout his life. Arnau is not portrayed as a very religious person, especially for the Middle Ages, but he identified as a Christian and held dear to him the Blessed Mother, personified to him by the Santa Maria del Mar statue.

Arnau's life is roughly contemporary with the construction of Santa Maria del Mar, 1329 through 1383. The church is made of thick stones that had to be carried from Möntjuic, the mountain on the other side of the city. Amy, Jessica, and I did not visit the quarry, but we did take a cable car from the beach at Barceloneta to a point midway up Möntjuic. It was a hot day and the remaining hike to the top of the mountain was not an easy one for me. Jessica was my angel that day: "Would you like a bottle of water? I took an extra one when I left the hotel." I can't believe I forgot to do the same. We came upon two dogs, one large and one small, chasing after a ball thrown by their master. This was, for me, a welcome break from the uphill climb, and I didn't have to admit how exhausted I was. The large dog would reach the ball first, but would almost always run past it wherein the little dog would scamper up and grab the ball. There were many people pausing on this hot day to watch those dogs, and it didn't matter if they spoke Spanish, Catalan, English, or French. We were all amused by those comical dogs. Eventually, the big dog got tired and jumped in a nearby fountain, while the little dog ran around the rim of the fountain, still taunting the big dog.

We eventually continued our ascent to the top of Möntjuic, finally arriving at the 17th-century castle on top. The views were outstanding: acres and acres of Barcelona with Gaudí's towering La Sagrada Familia easily visible among the shorter buildings. We took our photos from the top of the castle and decided we were too hot and tired to walk down the mountain and across the city to our hotel near Santa Maria. Amy saw them first: tourists leaving a taxi free for us! We grabbed that cab and cruised down the mountain which no longer seemed so steep and high. When I think of that day now, as I read Falcones's *Cathedral of the Sea*, I can't help but connect our taxi ride to the journey Arnau Estanyol and those other laborers made over approximately the same route, bent over with the heavy basilica stones on their backs.

Once his father died, young fictional Arnau was invited to join the *bastaixos*, and felt that he had to prove himself with heavy loads so that he could eventually be admitted into the bastaix guild. Some of the laborers were concerned for him because he was still a boy, and knowing of his devotion to Santa Maria, his substitute mother, sent him to clean his beloved chapel in order to give his back a rest and be in her presence.

It seemed absurd to me that three of my four most memorable sites in Barcelona were churches: La Sagrada Familia, Santa Maria del Mar, and the Basilica at Montserrat. Of course architect Antonio Gaudí's magnificent La Sagrada Familia cathedral would make the list. That place is breathtaking. It's no surprise that the modernist Palau de la Música Catalana would be the fourth place on the list, with its stained-glass auditorium, tiled columns, and bas-relief terracotta stage statues. Built between 1905 and 1908 by Antoni Gaudí's teacher, Lluís Domènech I Montaner, it's like no other concert venue I've seen. My friends and I attended a Flamenco performance in there. As magnificent as those dancers were, I was still distracted by the Palau's interior. The real surprise to me is that Santa Maria del Mar is on that list of most memorables. This working man's church with its sea theme gave me a feeling of calm and serenity. Maybe it was the maritime motifs which reminded me of home. Perhaps it was the enormous stones which make up the walls of the cathedral. I read once that bank architects liked to use big stones like this in the first half of the twentieth century to instill essential feelings of confidence in their customers. Those big cathedral blocks, carried here on the backs of laborers like Arnau all the way from the Möntjuic quarry, gave me confidence in this church along with serenity. This is a special place.

BARCELONETA: BEACH THROWS

On one free afternoon after a morning writing seminar, I planned to visit the beach at Barceloneta that I had seen from the cable car ride. It was that bird's eye view that convinced me to go. Of course when I returned to the hotel to drop off my books and change into my bathing suit, the maid was cleaning my room. One look from her communicated to me that no changing would take place until she was finished. I am intimidated by hotel maids, especially when I don't speak their language. I took off for the beach as-is, in shorts and T-shirt rather than purple slimming swimsuit. Luckily, I had tucked my new Barcelona-bought beach throw with flamingoes on it into my school bag just in case of such an event. I might look like a tourist on the Barceloneta beach, but I was a tourist with something beach-appropriate to sit on and a bag full of...books and notebooks. Nerd.

I was struck by how similar the area around the beach was to New Jersey beaches. There were casual restaurants, bars, beach supply stores, and hotels. There were families, young adults on skateboards, and kids. I sat on the beach for a couple of hours, with a book in my hands, but I was watching the vendors vending, the people sunning, and the young Catalan men stopping to chat up the extremely fair and blonde Scandinavian exchange students seated in front of me. (Whatever they said to the men ended each attempt at conversation definitively.) From my spot on my flamingo beach throw, I could have purchased cervezas, mojitos, water, massages, and round or rectangular beach throws (not blankets or towels but beautiful border printed fabric with or without fringe). This was different from my usual Cape May beach with no vendors. I bought none of these things.

When I went down to the water to put my feet into the Mediterranean Sea, I reached down to pick up a small, smooth, reddish stone which stays on my dresser now except when I'm reading *Cathedral of the Sea*. I turn its smoothness over in my hand as I read. Truth be told, I did buy another beach throw that day. Although I already bought the rectangular flamingo throw, I liked these round ones, about six feet in diameter, and promised myself if I saw a round one with elephants on it I'd spend the fifteen Euros. On the way back to the hotel, I saw a black and white throw with elephants marching in circles. It looks more Indian than Catalan because it was, in fact, made in India. It looks like Barcelona to me, however, and reminds me of that afternoon at the beach and putting my feet in the Mediterranean Sea.

MONTSERRAT: THE THIMBLE

Our group of writers boarded a small bus named "Dumbo" for our trip to Montserrat. We knew there was a mountain involved, and a monastery (another Santa Maria, this one of Montserrat with a Benedictine Abbey attached), and, we would lunch on top of the mountain. It seemed like a pleasant way to spend the afternoon and I was happy to be led around and told what's what on Montserrat. I would be sorry that I didn't do my usual compulsive advance research, though, as I missed my chance to see a mysterious medieval marvel called La Moraneta.

The Dumbo bus with the elephant on the side took us out of the city of Barcelona and into the suburbs of Catalonia. The enormous mountain came into view and there was no question why it was named Monstserrat or "Serrated Mountain." Its many rocky peaks form a jagged skyline and I wondered how the Dumbo bus would navigate the bumpy, hilly sides or serrations of the mountain. The ride up was thrilling: steep and curvy on a narrow road. Dumbo climbed for 15 to 20 minutes before we arrived at a busy reception area. This is where our group was ushered into the buffet restaurant where nothing was labeled. With my seafood allergy, I was afraid to eat many of the selections and ended up at the children's spread for some safe, reliable chicken fingers. Fortified, I set out with the others to explore the monastery.

The abbey was burned twice by Napoleon's troops

in 1811 and 1812. Twenty-two monks were killed by Republican forces. The abbey was closed for restoration from 1835 to 1844, so chances are what I thought were carefully-preserved medieval architectural elements were not. Still, the abbey is sumptuous. The monastery was closed during the Spanish Civil War, but during the rule of Francisco Franco it was known as a sanctuary and safe place for artists, scholars, politicians, and students.

I learned later in my souvenir book that the ornate Basilica houses a museum with paintings by the Spanish masters El Greco, Dali, and Picasso. There used to also be a publishing house there which published its first book in 1499. I noticed the many chandeliers hanging in the dark church. Each was different and was created from various metals and natural materials such as animal horns. "I wonder if they represent or commemorate something," Amy said, reading my mind. Although the mysterious fixtures were pictured in my souvenir book, there was no accompanying description.

There were storms in the area and we heard thunder in the distance. Short but torrential showers periodically delayed our explorations. After touring the monastery we trusted that no more rain would fall and set out with a smaller group of seven or eight for an easy hike to a lone mountaintop cross visible from the abbey. Forgetting about my aversions to steep ascents and high altitudes, I joined this group and made it about halfway up the trail before my lungs became fatigued and my breathing squeaky. I sat on a stone wall to rest. I decided to discontinue my ascent, but I didn't want my friends to spend even a minute wondering where I might be. I crafted a goofy text message: "Do not look for me atop the mountain, for I have descended. I'm on a bench beside the gift shop near the stairs." And there I sat reading my souvenir book about Montserrat like the travel nerd that I am.

It was then, on that bench, that I learned about the twelfth century Black Madonna, or La Moraneta. This is a sculpture of the Madonna and Child housed in the basilica, mere steps from where I was sitting. This statue is an important artifact from the Middle Ages which inspires actual pilgrimages. How could I miss this? This is the kind of Madonna statue where her seated body provides a throne on which the Christ child sits. These were common in the Middle Ages. Over the years, the faces and hands of the figures have darkened and even been painted black at times. The 38-inch statue sits in a room behind the altar and visitors stand in line to climb up stairs into the room. Why didn't I research this location? I would so rather have waited in that Black Madonna pilgrimage line than go on that uphill hike in scorching hot weather. It was too late to get in line now, and I missed my memorable medieval moment.

Back in the gift shop while I waited for the hikers, I saw a curious display of various styles and shapes of souvenir thimbles. This is curious because it's old-fashioned. Souvenir thimbles are hard to come by these days. I sew, so I notice them. What do thimbles have to do with Montserrat, monasteries, or Madonnas? It's a non-sequitur, but no matter. I didn't have to buy a thimble. But then I saw a basket full of owl-shaped metal thimbles with Black Madonna badges on their chests. I like owls, my college mascot was an owl, but what do owls have to do with serrated mountains and medieval Madonnas? The triple-non-sequitur peculiarity of this item compelled me to buy one. It sits on my coffee table now to remind me of the importance of researching places before I go, even when the excursion has been carefully planned by others, so as to not miss magical medieval moments.

HOME: THE BRACELET

Besides the medieval interest which attracted me, La Moraneta has obvious Marian interest, as in "of Mary."I recently read Beverly Donofrio's popular memoir, *Riding in Cars with Boys*, which details her colorful young adulthood. The follow-up to this book is another memoir, *Looking for Mary: (Or, the Blessed Mother and Me)*, which describes Donofrio's fascination/obsession with the Blessed Mother, AKA Santa Maria, AKA Mary. It all started with the purchase of a Madonna and Child statue at an estate sale. That statue turned into collection of Madonna statues, daily prayings of the Rosary, and ultimately attendance at a Marian retreat. I heard Donofrio speak about this memoir and I was struck by how the brash voice of *Riding in Cars* became reverent with a splash of mansuetude when she spoke about Mary. I've heard of people, some authors, in fact, who have returned to the Roman Catholic faith after years of detachment from it. Donofrio's experience was directed specifically at Mary, though, and she was sincere about how this devotion enriched her life. I was fascinated by Donofrio's talk, and later captivated by her book, *Looking for Mary*. Is this what I need, to be saying a Rosary every day? Was Mary reaching out to me through Santa Maria del Mar and La Moraneta?

During the time I was reading Beverly Donofrio's *Looking for Mary*, I described my Mary fascination to a friend. I suggested maybe we should be saying Rosaries to solve the problems vexing us. Rather than laughing nervously at my unexpected suggestion or changing the subject, he offered that when he prays he asks for guidance and strength rather than the actual solution to the problem. I agreed that this was the best prayer strategy and matched what my mother taught me. I remember the surprise I felt that he would let me in on this most private aspect of his life.

Anyway, this is how I always approached praying, but since my mother died I have never spoken about praying to anyone. I could feel our friendship knitting together through this brief conversation while sitting on a stone wall in the autumn sunshine. I felt like Mary herself was reaching out to me through my friend, confirming that yes, it was her at Santa Maria del Mar and at Montserrat, bringing my attention to those medieval monuments even though I hadn't actually made the pilgrimage to La Moraneta. Now that my mother is dead, should I take a page from fictional Arnaud Estanyol's book and claim a holy substitute mom in the very same way that he did in *Cathedral of the Sea*?

Soon after this conversation about praying, I happened to notice a Blessed Mother bracelet for sale online. It was simply a silver bangle with a sideways Mary medal soldered to it. I stared at it thinking that this could be another installment of Mary's message. If I bought this bracelet, how would I explain my wearing of religious jewelry? Why would I have to explain it? Who would dare ask?

I bought the bracelet and wore it. As if she knew I was struggling with how to explain her presence on my wrist, Mary planted a line in my head. (I think it was Mary.) If anyone asked about the bracelet, I would say, "I'm wearing this bracelet which features the Blessed Mother to remind me to be more compassionate." It is effective, by the way. I find myself rubbing my finger over the figure of Mary in times of anxiety when I don't know how to respond to things. She brings comfort. She also reminds me of those sunny days exploring Barcelona, missing out on seeing La Moraneta in Montserrat, and reading about Arnau Estanyol and Santa Maria del Mar during winter months in New Jersey.

Margaret Montet

Defending the Waltz King

He's probably Austria's favorite son, but his iconic golden statue is definitely the favorite among all the composer monuments at Vienna's Stadtpark.

"You know, that was just *entertainment*; that wasn't high art." And so it started: the young man behind us on the bus apparently did not enjoy the Strauss/ Mozart concert we attended as an optional excursion from our week-long river cruise. He continued: "You can tell because the orchestra was smaller. The Cleveland (Orchestra) is much bigger and they play pieces forty minutes long sometimes at their concerts. I've heard them five or six...or six or seven times. I heard them play Disney music." He was criticizing the small orchestra, but more so the musical selections of the evening. The same guy who respects Disney movie music could not accept the enduring melodic invention and exquisite orchestrations of a true innovator named Johann Strauss.

The young man's criticisms were especially obnoxious to me because I had just recently overcome my own prejudices against the Strauss family and sorted out who's who. Knowing that I would be visiting Vienna twice this summer, I wanted to know more about this famous family of waltz and light-music composers that I had been taught to ignore as a college music major. Perhaps stern Professor Parker said something like, "We do not study the music of Johann Strauss in this classroom. You must realize that it is not serious art music and not worth our attention." That's the kind of edict she would issue in our Music History III course often. I did not dare pay attention to Johann Strauss for decades. Here in Vienna, though, Strauss's music, portrait and name are found everywhere. Now with a group of writers for my second Viennese visit, I find myself staying in, of all places, the Johan Strauss

Hotel. In-between lectures and seminars, I visited the famous golden statue of Strauss in the Stadtpark and the Kursalon, the concert hall where Strauss conducted many concerts.

There's not a lot written about the Strausses besides brief encyclopedia entries, but I found a couple of scholarly articles and a fine collection of their waltzes, polkas, and marches with impressive album notes. My new Strauss compact discs received a lot of play in recent months and I began to wonder why waltzes make us want to waltz. It's counterintuitive, really, because waltzes have three beats in a measure, and most humans have two feet. I haven't found the answer to this, but the quest has been most delightful. While in Vienna, I even found time to visit his apartment, now a museum.

The musical Strausses captivated greater Vienna for almost a century. The first musical Strauss was Johann, born in 1804. He came from Leopoldstadt, a suburb of Vienna, and his father was a tavern owner. Johann's father died while Johann was young, and his mother married an innkeeper. This innkeeper stepfather tried to steer young Johann away from a career in music and into an apprenticeship in either bookbinding (or bookkeeping depending on who you read). Strauss loved music, though, and managed to learn how to play the viola well enough to abandon his apprenticeship at age fifteen and join an orchestra at a restaurant. Back in those days in Vienna, cafes, beer gardens, and other restaurants sponsored their own orchestras or bands much like the concept of the modern "house band." By 1819, Strauss and his friend

Josef Lanner were ready to go off on their own and start their own orchestra led by Lanner. They played at inns, ballrooms, and dance halls besides the usual cafes and beer gardens, and they became so popular around Vienna that they formed two orchestras, one led by Strauss, and the other by Lanner.

So you see, young man on the bus, these Strauss waltzes and marches and polkas were meant to be *entertainment*, light music, played by a small orchestra that would fit in a restaurant or ballroom. This was music created to add joy to the lives of the people of the greater Vienna area and inspire them to dance. Johann Strauss was an innovator, really, taking the idea of this new dance step and transforming it into an iconic musical form.

Then the inevitable happened. Strauss and Lanner had a tiff (creative differences, maybe?) and Strauss began his own orchestra. Around this time he had started composing waltzes which became popular, and in 1830 his band secured a gig at a beer garden and dance hall in Leopoldstadt called Sperlsaal, or "Sperl" for short. Sperl was a destination for foreign travelers, and soon word of Johann Strauss and his waltzes spread beyond Vienna and even Austria, and Strauss took his orchestra on the road. He continued to compose waltzes, marches, and polkas along with other short dance forms and built his fame, fortune, and confidence.

Just before the orchestra's popularity took off, in 1825, Strauss married a woman named Anna Streim. By all accounts, she was a good partner for him and encouraged his remarkable musical career, both as a performer and a composer. Three sons appeared on the scene: Johann II in 1825, Josef in 1827, and Eduard in 1835. All three showed musical promise, but Strauss the father did not want musical careers for them. Johann the younger wrote his first waltz at age six and wanted to follow in his father's footsteps. He secretly took violin lessons from a member of his father's band, but when he became of age found himself in a bank job thanks to Johann the father. The son Johann was miserable, but opportunity presented itself in the most unusual way.

Remember how we believed Johann Strauss the elder when he said he was off touring with his orchestra in other parts of Europe? That was partly true, but he was also leading a double life with a mistress and their five children together! He left Anna to live in comfort with Emilie Trampusch, a wealthy widow, while his first, legal, family lived a meager existence. Johann the Younger saw his opening, appealed to his mother, the deserted and devastated Anna, and she set him up with proper music lessons. By age 19, he formed his own orchestra which debuted at Dommayer's Restaurant in Heitzing. His program included one of his father's waltzes, *Strains of the Lorelei and the Rhine*, and a new waltz of his own. Johann the Elder could not attend because he was ill at his ladyfriend's house, but word of his son's triumph made it back to the father. Johann the Younger's fame spread rapidly as his orchestra and original compositions were even better than his father's. (Sometimes Johann I got carried away trying to thrill audiences with fancy violin stunts that did not fit the purpose of the dance music.) The son is the

Johann we recognize today as "The Waltz King," not the father.

There was not to be a reconciliation of the Johanns but there was a reconciliation of the orchestras. Johann the Elder died from scarlet fever in 1849 with Johann the Younger at his bedside, and was laid to rest in Vienna with thousands attending his funeral. Johann the Younger, The Waltz King, combined the two orchestras and toured extensively in Europe.

So my question remains: why all the traditional negativity towards the Strausses and the waltz? Even on our cruise ship, while the program director was presenting a brief program on another Austrian son, Mozart, the director's narration bumbled over to Johann Strauss, The Waltz King. "I really don't like Strauss, though. I do like another Viennese composer named Gustav Mahler." How can a cruise professional on a cruise named "The Danube Waltz" stand there and profess a distaste for the musical innovator who made the waltz a Vienna institution? This prejudice can't be simply because the waltz is a shorter form and geared toward dancing. Could it possibly be because there was some scandal surrounding this new dance? Some straight-laced Viennese were shocked at how close the couple stands and how the man was expected to put his arm around the lady's waist. Nonetheless, the scandalous waltz made its way into serious concert literature, either as a standalone such as Ravel's *La Valse* or Chopin's and Brahms's waltzes for piano, and as a popular choice for symphonic movements (Berlioz's *Symphonie Fantastique!*). Maybe it was the Strausses themselves who, in spite of their raging popularity in Vienna, caused societies influenced by England's strait-laced Queen Victoria to gasp in horror. (Queen Victoria's reign began in 1837.)

Maybe I have something there. Johann Strauss the Younger had his own romance and marriage problems. Somewhere in his early romantic career, there was an affair with Olga Smirnitskaya, a Russian noblewoman. He met her during the summers he spent near St. Petersburg. His *Waltz Reiseabenteuer* tells the story of their relationship. He quoted vignettes from it in letters he wrote to Olga. (His letters survive, by the way, but hers do not.) Their love was doomed because her parents did not approve. That was that.

During his marriage to his first wife, Henriette Treffz, Johann II cut down on the touring and only did a few very special concerts. Jetty, as she was known, was an operatic mezzo-soprano who had been the mistress of a wealthy businessman named Eduard Todesco. She had seven children out of wedlock, and they were not all necessarily Todesco's. She was seven years older than her husband, but as we'll see, age is just a number to him. During Jetty's marriage to Johann Strauss the Younger, she insisted that he tour less and compose more. He did exactly that in the 1860s and early 1870s. *Bluette Polka Française*, Op. 271 from 1862 was dedicated to her. She exposed him to theater music, especially opera and operetta. Jetty died of a heart attack in 1877.

I visited the apartment where the Strausses lived. Inside those high-ceilinged, dark-wood-paneled rooms, Johann and Jetty could look out on the fashionable boulevard called the Praterstrasse and watch the pedestrian and carriage traffic. Today the apartment showcases Strauss's piano, violin, dance cards, a lock of Jetty's curly dark hair, and scores of scores and newspapers.

After Jetty died, Johann the Younger married Angelika Dittrich ("Lili"), a young actress twenty-five years younger than himself. The age difference was one problem, but Angelika was an embarrassingly loose woman during their marriage, referred to even as a strumpet! (When was the last time you heard someone called a strumpet??) Johann divorced her after five years of turmoil, sort of. The Roman Catholic Church would not give him a divorce, so he and wife number three became Lutherans. Before things got rotten with Lili, he dedicated the *Kuss-Walzer*, Op. 400, (The "Kiss Waltz") to her.

Adèle Deutsch became Johann's third wife. Although thirty-one years younger, she was a companion and inspiration to him. She encouraged his composition and was rewarded with a dedication for her thirtieth birthday, the *Adèlen-Walzer*, Op. 424.

There's a painting in the lobby of Vienna's Johann Strauss Hotel that catches my eye every time I walk by it. It is a portrait of Johann Strauss the Younger in formal white tie. His prominent black mustache is wider than his face and almost wider than his dyed black hair. (Multiple sources agree that he dyed his hair black to retain a youthful look.) His dark eyes stare back at the viewer with a kind gaze, and multiple couples waltz behind him. It's the same recognizable face one sees all over Vienna. Imagine how difficult it would be for a musician to attain that distinction in this musical city, known as the home of Haydn, Mozart, Beethoven, Schubert, Bruckner, Brahms, Mahler, and Schoenberg.

Strauss would ultimately compose over five hundred dances and sixteen operettas (including *Die Fledermaus*, *A Night in Venice*, and *Carnival in Rome*) which dominated his later years. He's credited with moving the spirit of the waltz from the country beer garden to the sophisticated city concert hall as a brilliant, expressive musical form. So I guess the young guy on the bus was right about the early waltz, but probably doesn't realize that other composers carried it forth into more recent literature.

There's more to the Strauss Family story. Josef Strauss, the middle brother born in 1827, was a quiet, intelligent kind of kid. His father wanted him to go into the army, but his ideas didn't fit with that. He studied to become an engineer instead. He was content with his engineering career, playing in amateur musical groups on the side, until brother Johann became exhausted and needed a substitute. Josef hesitated to leave his comfortable existence as an engineer, but consented to temporarily take control of the Strauss orchestra. He became popular in his new role and would compose over 280 waltzes, polkas, mazurkas, and quadrilles (all dances). He died young, at age 43. Some writers say his compositions had more depth and emotion than Johann's.

Eduard, the baby brother born in 1835, debuted as a conductor at age 24. He also composed, but excelled as a conductor. He and Josef took over the conducting work for Johann when Johann was married to the demanding Jetty. When Josef died in 1870, Eduard (known as Edi) began squiring the Strauss Orchestra all over the world including to American centenary celebrations. The Strauss brothers often collaborated on their compositions, borrowing each other's ideas to develop and revise. The *Trifolien Waltzer* and *Schützen Quadrille* are two examples of Strauss collaboration. Have you been to a grade school orchestra concert lately? *The Pizzicato Polka*, frequently featured on such programs in a watered-down version, started its life as a collaboration between Johann II and Josef.

The death of Johann in 1899 brought on the end of this waltz era. The orchestra disbanded in 1901. The sometimes-harsh music critic Eduard Hanslick said in his obituary for Johann Strauss II, "Along with him we have lost the most original musical talent of Vienna." Knowing all of this history, who would disagree? Hanslick continued: "His melodic invention flowed as delightfully as it was inexhaustible, his rhythms pulsated in lively exchange; harmony and form remained pure and straightforward."

Johann Strauss's death mask is on display in the apartment on the Praterstrasse. Approaching it, I felt an uncomfortable chilly feeling, probably because I was in the midst of my study of the man and his career. That chill intensified as I noticed his teeth were visible beneath the famous mustache (teeth don't usually show in a death mask, do they?), and oh, his right eyelid is slightly open. I looked away. I looked back. I looked away, and finally returned my gaze to this mask of the Maestro's face. I was fascinated.

Strauss the Waltz King was an original, and musicians appreciate him still, especially in Vienna. Scholarship on the Strauss legacy is centered at the Wiener Stadt- und Landesbibliothek, or Vienna City Library, the home of the world's largest Strauss archive. Initiatives there and in conjunction with those musical professionals include:

- a definitive multi-volume set of the collected works of Johann Strauss II,
- *the Strauss – Elementar Verzeichnis*, a three-volume reference catalogue listing Strauss's works by genre and opus number,
- a scholarly journal named *Der Fledermaus*.

This scholarly activity would seem to give the Strauss family, especially Johann Strauss II, some credibility and gravitas. But the Strauss saga is not over; there are more scandals to come. Most of the musical works in this archive are sketches and notebooks rather than complete works. It seems Eduard Strauss had custody of the Strauss Orchestra's archive since 1870 and he had much of it burned! We don't know why for sure, but some experts believe he resented not being mentioned in Johann II's will. Other scholars suggest that Eduard and Josef had a pact to burn the works of whoever died first. Eduard did this, mostly, but saved a few pieces that he really loved. By then, some were already in print and preserved for the future.

And then there's this not-so-well-kept secret: not every note of Strauss music was written by the Strausses. During the time of Johann Strauss I, it was a fully accepted practice to engage in teamwork when putting together light concert music. Guys in the band would contribute ideas and melodies similar to how jazz musicians work today. In Johann Strauss's milieu, this was less accepted, both because artists were more concerned with ownership, and because Strauss II was functioning on a more professional world stage.

Evidently, chunks of the *Die Fledermaus* score in the archive is in musician Richard Genée's handwriting. In light of my new Strauss fan girl status, I would like to think there is a reasonable explanation for this. Could Richard Genée have been picking up a few extra bucks copying for the Maestro? This was a common practice up until the days of digitally printed sheet music. I prefer to think this is the case. We will never know for sure because so many of the manuscripts were burned, but consider that Johann Strauss the Younger was the artistic leader of this waltzing endeavor, and he had high standards anyone composing would have had to meet.

No matter what the critics and scholars say, I prefer to represent the listeners: the musical dilettantes and the ballroom dancers. The music composed by the members of the Strauss Family is a delight and representative of the Romantic Era in Vienna. It seems to sparkle during the fleeting moments it exists in the air around the listener. "What more can we ask of music?" is what I should have asked that opinionated young man on the bus…and Professor Parker.

Margaret Montet

Molto Vivace Vienna

Mozart composed some of his most famous later works in this house, but today the exterior of the Mozarthaus seems to fade into the Vienna scenery.

I walked past the white-wigged Mozarts in fancy court dress selling concert tickets to tourists and found my way into the Opera. This was my first day in Vienna. Our tour guide walked us through the ornate "interval" (intermission) rooms, the auditorium, and the stage. For the rest of my stay, I got my bearings for music-themed Vienna excursions at the enormous Vienna State Opera, which, as luck would have it, was only a few blocks from my hotel. The opera house was the Habsburg emperor Franz Joseph's brainchild, built to impress anyone who visited Vienna. Emperor Franz Joseph's interval room is available for fancy parties these days, but back when he was around this is where he would spend his time. He did not like opera, so he hid out here during performances. The Sacher Hotel, home of the delectable Sacher Torte (chocolate with apricot filling) is across from the Opera House. The Karlsplatz subway station with its station house designed by *fin de siècle* architect Otto Wagner is nearby, waiting to transport me to further-flung destinations. After my explorations, I could usually find my way through the city back to this enormous opera house, and then to the yellow corner café with the gelato take-out window which signaled a left turn to the hotel. If I saw the pink pastry café (one of a chain of cafés called *Aïda*) where I ate that luscious strawberry tart, or the café with the red umbrellas where I had the crispy deep-fried *Weiner Schnitzel* on my first day, I would know I had gone too far.

Besides the grand Vienna State Opera, the many theaters, composer statues, and Museum of Sound, there are three composers' apartments curated to show the visitor how these musicians lived. Vienna's musical history was definitely on my mind during my visit because I was preparing to teach a course on the topic to the culturally sophisticated residents at a certain retirement village back home. On the last day of a course I called "The Evolution of the Symphony," in which the city of Vienna popped up repeatedly, my students expressed a desire for another course in a similar style. "I'll be in Vienna for two weeks this summer," I said, "How about I put together a course on the music of that city?" I saw their faces brighten as soon as the words were out of my mouth, and course registrations flooded in soon after.

This would not merely be another Music History course, but music mixed with travel for a population who mostly could no longer travel themselves. I would be doing the legwork for them and presenting a three-week multimedia musical Viennese travelogue upon my return. It may sound nerdy, but having a purpose or quest in mind before a trip adds to my anticipation. I was curious to find out how Vienna presents its fantastic musical history to visitors, and this is how I would focus this huge subject for my students at the retirement village.

These students I attempt to enlighten at the Village are an exuberant group. Many have some kind of physical limitation and have acquired canes, walkers, or motorized scooters since I've known them. Their enthusiasm for learning has not diminished. They are well-read, well-listened, and well-traveled, and I would not step in front of them without a thorough knowledge of the subject at hand. Their questions are thoughtful and intelligent, and they have been known to stump me on occasion. (They appreciate when I research their questions and bring answers to the next class.) Just as in high school, there are noticeable leaders. In this situation, they are not varsity athletes, cheerleaders, or debate team captains, but the folks responsible for curating the array of programs, lectures, courses, workshops, and activities available to these lifelong learners. Some participants in this course had been to Vienna long ago, maybe with a spouse now gone. A few were looking forward to upcoming trips. Nevertheless, as I prepared for this course, I felt as if I was traveling for them as their eyes and ears in 21st-century Vienna.

I didn't worry about getting lost finding Mozart's apartment. (Let me be clear: this museum is called the Mozart Museum, Mozart's Apartment, *MozartWohnung*, or *Figarohaus*. There are four names for the same destination.) I studied my tourist map and realized I simply had to locate the immense St. Stephen's Cathedral, a short distance from the Opera House. The altar-end of the cathedral (the apse) points to *Figarohaus* a few blocks away. Once in the neighborhood, there were many signs featuring Mozart's familiar face to guide me to this destination. Now known mostly as the *Figarohaus*, this apartment is where Wolfgang A. Mozart lived for two and a half years while he was composing his blockbuster opera, *The Marriage of Figaro*. I described later the Maestro's home where he composed *Figaro* during the Mozart opera segment of the course, and the students were riveted. None had been. Mozart's home, along with the two floors above, comprised the imaginative museum.

Now, I don't mean to say that *Figarohaus* did not meet my expectations. Rather, I would like to express that it did not *match* my expectations. The rooms are sparsely furnished with a few items "from the time of Mozart" in order to give the visitor an *idea* of what the rooms were used for. No furniture known to have belonged to Mozart has survived. The documents displayed behind glass are mostly facsimiles, again to give an idea of Mozart's life. Multimedia displays tell the story of Mozart's life and compositions in his later years, but he'd have moved to another apartment nearby before he died at age 35. The real museum is the collection of rooms of the Mozart apartment, still in the same configuration they were in at the time that Mozart, his wife Constanze, and their two sons lived here. I knew as I looked out Mozart's window onto the Blutgasse (Blood Alley!), that I would be sharing this moment with my students. This view was Mozart's view.

Many now-famous composers transplanted themselves to Vienna (Wolfgang Mozart from Salzburg, Ludwig van Beethoven, and Johannes Brahms from Germany) because of the arts-supporting Habsburg dynasty. Other composers (Richard Wagner and Giaochino Rossini) visited briefly, enjoying important premieres of their work in Vienna's theaters. Johann Strauss, father and son, Anton Bruckner, and Franz Schubert were born in the city or nearby and could take advantage of the city's musical resources from the time they were children.

There is no easy trick to finding Vienna native

Johann Strauss II's apartment on the *Praterstrasse*, the once-fashionable boulevard leading to the park with the 212-foot-high *Riesenrad*, (Ferris wheel). Luckily I had the exact street address handy or I would never been able to find the Strauss house. There is but a tiny sign on the door leading to the second floor apartment/museum, and this door is in the walkway to the building's courtyard. There is a slightly bigger sign on the door to the actual museum. I didn't notice the commemorative plaque until I was back outside. I included the story of my arduous journey to Johann Strauss's house when I taught the group about Strauss's waltzes and operettas. By then it had become comic.

The Strauss Wohnung does not have the fancy interactive multimedia displays that *Figarohaus* has, but it does have listening stations and genuine artifacts:

- Johann Strauss's pianos—he wasn't known as a pianist, but he probably used these instruments (a grand and an upright) to work out those catchy melodies and find the perfect harmonies for those lively (*vivace!*) waltzes, polkas, marches, and operettas.
- His violin—Imagine the stories this violin could tell! Strauss had his violin with him on the podium from his *Biergarten* dance orchestra days to the celebrated concert engagements. It's kept in a glass case to keep fingers like mine from touching it.
- A lock of his first wife Netty's hair—I wonder what his second and third wives thought about him saving this artifact.

Margaret Montet

- Newspaper clippings, awards, and photographs from the Waltz King's life well-lived, all captioned in German. (Why did I not throw that German-English dictionary into my bag for this excursion?)
- As with the *Figarohaus*, the apartment itself is an exhibit in this museum. Look out Strauss's window and you're looking down on the *Praterstrasse*, a fashionable boulevard during Strauss's time here. His view would have been the same, except for the motorized traffic.

The item which elicited my most powerful reaction is at the end of the exhibit. It's the death mask. Strauss's teeth are visible—isn't that unusual for a death mask? And then I noticed that one of his eyelids is partially open. *It's creepy but natural,* I thought, but I was not able to forget it. Should I tell my elderly students about the death mask, I wondered? I decided not to decide yet, but to wait until that moment in the Village's Game Room/classroom when I would describe the Strauss artifacts.

The third *Wohnung* composer home in Vienna is Beethoven's *Pasqualatihaus*, named for his landlord. Beethoven has been my favorite composer since I can remember. Time was limited on this trip, though, and I had to make some tough choices. I reminded myself of my quest: "How does Vienna present its musical history?" With so many composers creating music in Vienna (Mozart, Strauss I, Strauss II, Schubert, Bruckner, Haydn, and Mahler), it's probably best to focus on the native Austrians, and of those, the individuals most revered in Vienna. But I had been expecting to visit some Beethoven sites, and I suspected my students at the Village were expecting some Beethoven, too. Someday I will embark upon a Beethoven-themed Vienna visit which will include the *Pasqualatihaus*, the Beethoven statue, Beethoven's grave, and Heiligenstadt where he wrote that poignant letter to his brothers when he realized he was going deaf. That letter has given music historians a glimpse of Beethoven's mind for centuries, so a trip out to his apartment in Heiligenstadt would be inspiring. How can I get Beethoven into this course when I haven't visited these important places? Would this omission threaten my credibility with the Village students?

Once back at my desk at home, I found a way. I made it up to Beethoven by doing some meticulous research on the surprisingly shoddy orchestras he had to work with and his role in the evolution of conducting. The articles I found were full of examples of I-bet-you-didn't-know-THIS information. For example, once royal Hapsburg support slowed to a trickle, musicians in Beethoven's day were paid so poorly they had to take multiple gigs. The resulting orchestras were poor. When a conflict came up they would hire an inferior substitute to take their place at one of the jobs. In spite of these challenges and his increasing hearing loss, Beethoven was the greatest symphonic innovator we've known. My students were surprised that Beethoven was the first conductor to stand in front of the orchestra with a stick of some kind. Before his time, the orchestra's first chair violinist or the piano soloist would conduct from their seat with

a violin bow, a chin, or a free hand. The only time a
conductor stood in front of the orchestra was when a
chorus was also involved. Beethoven liked the control
he had while standing in front. I demonstrated how he
would crouch down low for the soft parts and reach
for the ceiling when leading the loud parts. He did
more than just beat time.

I would have missed an important Beethoven
landmark if my classmate, Mark, had not pointed it
out. A bunch of us had gone to the Naschmarket
neighborhood one evening for dinner. There were six
or seven of us, or eight or nine, and with that many
diners there's bound to be some negotiations about
location. While negotiations were taking place, Mark
and I were looking around at the scenery. He spotted
the sign for the Theater an der Wien, just a block away.
This was the venue for so many premieres of now-
canonic symphonies, operas, and plays. It takes its
name from the Wien River which used to flow past
the theater but is now covered up by the Naschmarket.
The most famous concert to take place here was
a Beethoven "Academy" on December 22, 1808.
Beethoven premiered his Fifth and Sixth symphonies,
the Fourth Piano Concerto, and his Choral Fantasy
along with some smaller works. The heating system
was broken that cold December day, so the aristocratic
concertgoers shivered through four hours of music.
They got to hear Maestro Beethoven play the piano
for the concerto, but the orchestra was mediocre.
Many of the usual Theater an der Wien musicians were
performing at the nearby Burgtheater and filled their
Theater an der Wien chairs with whatever substitutes

they could get. The epic concert was well-received judging by the reviews that survive.

A day or two after the Naschmarket dinner, I attended a lecture by Dr. Cornelia Szabo-Knotik of the University of Vienna. My two hours in the role of a student at this lecture augmented my knowledge with countless "Austrian nuances" and behind-the-scenes information. It was an authentic student experience: as I copied down these pearls of wisdom, the student sitting next to me doodled with many colored pens her wish for additional sleep. Other students fidgeted, probably because technical problems prevented the professor from sharing visual aids, and her Austrian accent made her words difficult to decipher at times. It was a hot Vienna July day and the room was not air-conditioned. I empathized with the professor. At one of my former teaching venues, no one bothered to tell me there was no wifi for my "The Passion of Opera" course until I was setting up for the first class. I scrambled to locate some opera overtures and arias on YouTube with my smartphone. This was not optimal. I was able to ignore the Austrian professor's calamities because I was hearing the local perspective on Music History from an actual Austrian! The lecture helped me understand Vienna's musical heritage. The professor cleared up that Joseph Haydn did not acquire the nickname "Papa Haydn" simply because he lived to be an avuncular old man. German-speakers know the accent is on the second syllable making it "PaPA Haydn," and that this is an Austrian term of respect for one who excelled in his role as mentor. I never knew that. Shedding my teacher persona, I savored my role as a student, and looked forward to the authenticity this experience would bring to my own course.

The professor revealed another Austrian Music History nugget, this time about Johannes Brahms and Anton Bruckner: They hated each other. Though he was a transplant from Germany, Brahms found his way into the polite aristocratic Viennese society. Bruckner was a country-boy organist from Upper Austria who spoke with a heavy accent and had too many rough edges to hobnob with the fancy. He was obsessed with his Catholic religion and wrote religious music and symphonies injected with Austrian folk music. Unlike the popular Brahms, he was hated by the critics. He received some acclaim as a church organist and played at the palace chapel. Later on, when the trend toward Nationalism became vital in concert music, Bruckner's works received more attention.

Today we hear both Bruckner and Brahms at orchestral concerts and we're unaware that Bruckner was not part of the Viennese musician in-crowd. The Bruckner statue in the Stadtpark is a tribute for sure, but is it at the same time a tongue-in-cheek metaphor? This maestro is depicted climbing over a wall. How could that wall represent anything other than the Viennese aristocracy from which Bruckner was shut out all his life? This insight was golden for my Vienna course as none of my students knew anything about Bruckner's difficulty with Viennese society.

The professor focused on *fin de siècle* (end of the century) Vienna and hardly mentioned the Viennese Classicists Haydn, Mozart and Beethoven who were emphasized in my American musical education. The *fin de siècle* period is crucial to Viennese cultural memory because this is when Gustav Klimt and the Secessionist artists created their distinctive, innovative art, and Sigmund Freud invented modern psychoanalysis with the publication of *The Interpretation of Dreams*. That book was actually ready for publication in 1899, but Freud held off on it until 1900 so that it would usher in a new century of psychology.

In the musical universe, Gustav Mahler was raising the standards and growing the repertoire at the Imperial Opera House on the *Ringstrasse*. [The Ringstrasse is the wide boulevard which took the place of the city's medieval wall in the nineteenth century. Johann Strauss II wrote a polka to commemorate this event. The boulevard circles the older part of the city now, but used to divide the city from the suburbs. Emperor Franz Joseph had many important buildings erected on the *Ringstrasse* including the Kunsthistorisches (Art History) Museum, the Natural History Museum, and the gigantic Opera House.] Today we know Mahler as a composer of epic symphonies and orchestral song cycles, but in the *fin de siècle* Austrian Empire he made his name as an opera conductor. He changed how we attend opera performances by insisting that the house be darkened and no latecomers were to be admitted once the performance had started. He eliminated disruptive cheers for favorite opera stars. In a well-known quote, *"Tradition ist Schlamperei."* ("Tradition is sloppy.") Mahler is referring to this traditional rude behavior in the Opera House as sloppy. He required more rehearsals than in the past and often programmed music that had not been heard yet in Vienna. Mahler was a Jew who converted to Catholicism when he left his post at Budapest's Opera House for Vienna's, but anti-Semitism growing in Vienna nagged him for the ten years he spent on the *Ringstrasse*. He was treated poorly even though his musical contributions were recognized, finally resigning this post in 1907 for a new position at the Metropolitan Opera in New York. Vienna realized they had lost a true musical innovator and named a grandiose interval room after him. I was impressed by that room and the other tributes I saw on the Opera House tour. There was even a sculpture of Mahler by Auguste Rodin, a twin of the one I would view later in Philadelphia's Rodin Museum.

I thought I'd mastered French pronunciation after all of those years of study, but in Vienna, I was focusing on those long German words and sounds: *Kunsthistorisches* Museum, *Fruhlingstimmen Walzer*, *Gesamtkunstwerk, Sacher Torte, Zauberflöte.* My French was repressed, so I should have known to practice the one French term I needed there: *fin de siècle.* Practice: Say it slowly, say it quickly. Use it in sentences. I should have practiced so that when I had lunch with a favorite classmate in the *Stadtpark Biergarten* I wouldn't stumble over this one basic French phrase. It was a funny but humbling moment I wish never happened. I told this story to my students, playing up the correct pronunciation and then to their delight exaggerating my mispronunciation. It was one of the funniest moments we ever shared.

After that lunch in the *Biergarten*, I wandered through this precious free afternoon in the Stadtpark, photographing the statues of famous musicians there. First is the famous Johann Strauss II statue which depicts the Waltz King in gold under a white arch decorated by cherubs. Before finding the Franz Schubert statue in the park, my Nikon malfunctioned, but I didn't panic. I pulled out my smart phone, and used that camera. I crowd-sourced the error code from the DSLR camera and my buddy back at work looked it up to tell me how to adjust it in time for the next outing. (He could count it in his reference desk statistics.) Meanwhile, the Anton Bruckner, Franz Lehár, and Johannes Brahms monuments are waiting for their close-ups.

I read in preparation for this trip and in reaction to it, even a couple of mysteries set in this Queen of Cities. As usual, I learned about the city's history via its music and art, and my interest went beyond the course I was planning. I acquired books while there and learned about more Vienna-themed books and articles once I got home. I kept reading about Vienna months after the trip was over. I realized eventually that I had done exactly what Vienna wanted me to do. I visited the homes of the representatives of its two musical heydays, Mozart of the Classical, and Strauss of the *fin de siècle*. These were the locations most obvious to Vienna visitors, I think, and it was Strauss and Mozart music playing in the tourist shops, hotel breakfast rooms, Austrian Airways airplanes, and concerts designed for tourists. Beethoven, long my favorite, had been pushed out of my itinerary, and I rarely stumbled upon his music in the way I repeatedly heard Strauss waltzes and Mozart symphonies everywhere I went. I realized that Beethoven represents a period of Viennese history when music was not supported as much. He overcame those obstacles to become an unfading phenomenon, but still not one of Vienna's top two golden boys. It took me a while to figure this out.

The Vienna course, in case you're wondering, was a big hit. I was expecting to see maybe twenty students in the Village Game Room, and I found *twenty-five* eager students. Word-of-mouth travels swiftly in the Village. Some had been to Vienna and asked me if I had visited their favorite places: "Did you see the marionettes? The Lipizzaner Stallions? Schonbrunn Palace? Did you taste the Sacher Torte?" Those who hadn't been there enjoyed my photographs from the trip and my stories about the *Reisenrad* and the pastry shops. I chose the best twenty or so photos from the 1,600 that I took, and added a few more inspired by our discussions. One couple was planning a future trip and wanted some first-hand travel information. The course included parts of Vienna culture and history that I didn't know about until I visited the city: the long line of music-supporting Hapsburgs featuring Emperor Franz Joseph and Empress Maria Theresia, the Strauss Family, Mahler-as-conductor, and the *fin de siècle* scene. The students were fascinated by the Johann Strauss II death mask and the recyclable coffin I saw at the sumptuous Melk Abbey. This came up in the inevitable conversation about why Mozart was buried in a mass grave. Well, he wasn't, exactly. "Only the upper class got to keep their coffin for eternity and enjoy a private grave," I explained. "The regular folks got the no-frills version: a coffin with a hinged bottom and a *shared* grave. Once the musical genius hit the floor of his final resting place the coffin was taken away and used again." And the next week I projected the photo I took of such a coffin at Melk Abbey, just north on the Danube.

And how does one end such a course? Typically, I end my lectures with an inspiring image or video. After reflecting on my experiences, the places I visited, the people I met, and the books I read, I decided to represent my unexpected new-found fondness for the Waltz King, Johann Strauss II. I showed the class a recent New Year's Day video of the Vienna Philharmonic conducted by the charismatic Franz Welser-Möst. They perform Johann Strauss II's "Beautiful Blue Danube" with young Austrian ballet dancers in dreamy sequences intermingled with footage of the world-class musicians. This seemingly simple waltz, joyful and lighthearted, has become Austria's unofficial national anthem. For me it symbolizes Vienna better than any other piece of music or art or literature. We ended on a high note.

Margaret Montet

Enduring Images
of Kafka's Prague

*A tour group huddles to hear about Týn Church
(The Church of Our Lady Before Týn) in Old
Town Prague as a brief shower falls on their
umbrellas.*

As the café's Gypsy band played Frank Sinatra's "Fly Me to the Moon," my cousin's son proposed to his girlfriend and presented her with my Aunt Grace's antique engagement ring. Until I went there myself, this was the image that sprung to mind when anyone mentioned Prague, the "City of a Hundred Spires."

I looked forward to exploring Franz Kafka's Prague: Castle Hill, the medieval architecture, the maze-like city streets, the Charles Bridge over the Vltava River, the Old Town Square, and the Astronomical clock around the corner. Descriptions of the Castle intrigued me most before my sister and I arrived for our short stay. Up on a hill and visible from almost anywhere in the city, it is thought to be the inspiration for Franz Kafka's great novel, *The Castle*. My imagination went berserk reading about this castle and imagining it in a foggy twilight. (Would it be my most enduring memory from Prague?) Although he felt like an outsider all his life here, Kafka is central to the Prague experience. Here's an example of the twisty-turny Kafkaesque-ness of Kafka:

> You do not need to leave your room. Remain sitting at your table and listen. Do not even listen, simply wait. Do not even wait, be quite still and solitary. The world will freely offer itself to you to be unmasked, it has no choice, it will roll in ecstasy at your feet.

> Franz Kafka,
> "The Great Wall of China" (1917)

Our tour started in Prague's *Staré Město* or Old Town. While some of our group members scrambled to buy umbrellas for a rain shower that would last 15 minutes, I sat down on a curb in the Old Town Square to wait. This was Kafka's world. He spent most of his life living and working in buildings on the square with names like *U Radnice 5*, *Sixt House*, The House at the Three Kings, and *House U Minuty*. That last building has spectacular examples of Renaissance murals on the exterior featuring ivory-colored figures on a charcoal-grey background. The name means "at the minute" in Czech and refers to the small servings of tobacco that were once sold there. I saw the spot where Kafka was born in 1883, now the Kafka Café, adjacent to a shop that sells only pencils. There's a Kafka bookstore and numerous plaques commemorating buildings in which he lived. Kafka fans can go to the Kafka Center to get a map of the Kafka sites.

I watched as another tour group huddled around their guide, their multicolored unfurled umbrellas forming a roof over most of the group. I snapped a photo of this scene, with the Tyn Church's spires rising behind the group and the cobblestone pavement shiny from the rain. That photo of the umbrellas in Old Town Square would become my favorite photograph from Prague.

There were other things going on in Old Town Square as I was capturing my picture-perfect moment. To the left of me, three Segway riders tried to lure tourists on a Segway tour. To my right, emanating from some vendors' stalls, large soap bubbles rose to the clouds. Another pair of sisters in our group recommended a tubular pastry sold from a cart on the square: "These are to-die-for! But if a whole one is too much you can share like we did." And so we did, one evening after dinner. These pastries had no name from what I could tell except for "Bavarian Treat," and they were sold all over town. They are baked in long tubes on metal cylinders and cut down to about six inches for the customer. Chocolate is spread inside just before you eat it and the thing is still warm and fragrant. I could smell those pastries as I watched the people in the square.

There were brides being photographed on the square. Lots of brides, and all seemed to be Asian. I found out later that a popular South Korean television soap opera called, "Lovers in Prague," takes place right here in the Czech capital. Eighteen episodes aired in 2005 and fans still come to Prague's town hall to be married and pose in Old Town Square and in front of the iconic Astronomical Clock. We lost count at 25 brides that morning. Prague is still so important to those Korean fans that the Czech Republic has opened a tourist office in Seoul, South Korea's capital. I found the show on YouTube and watched a little bit. It's no *Downton Abbey*.

The most famous attraction near the square is the 15th-century Astronomical Clock. This mechanical marvel marks every hour with a grandiose show of chimes and a parade of twelve apostles inside the little windows above the clock. Please note also that the sun and moon revolve around the earth here, and Prague is the center of the earth. The zodiac signs were added in the 19th century. Our group got to watch the clock go through its top-of-the-hour machinations through a curtain of light rain. Kafka never wrote about clocks from what I can tell, but he would have walked past this one every day on his way to the Worker's Insurance Accident Institute where he worked as an insurance claims officer for fourteen years.

Our tour group eventually wound its way over hilly cobblestone streets to Prague Castle after checking out the architecture in Old Town. The castle is actually a megalopolis of smaller palaces, houses, and the imposing St. Vitus Cathedral, built over the centuries around Castle Square. From a distance it looks like one giant castle, grandly illuminated at night. Our group cruised through Castle Square, inside the main gate where we saw the guards change, and briefly stopped in St. Vitus Cathedral. (We were headed to swanky Lobkowicz Palace for a tour.) Visitors may buy a ticket to tour some of the other castle buildings, and see more of St. Vitus than just the free zone just before the nave. St. Vitus's stained glass windows are impressive, but the one most visitors crane their necks to see was created by Czech artist Alphonse Mucha. Without a ticket we could only see about half of it, even with some serious neck-craning. This cathedral is very important to Czech Catholics as many of their local saints and kings are entombed here. Kafka probably had St. Vitus in his head when he wrote chapter nine of his novel, *The Trial*. We were tempted to linger longer here, but we didn't want to miss the Lobkowicz Palace tour at which we were promised a fancy lunch and chamber music concert.

Defenestration. I heard this curious word often in

Prague. It means to be thrown out of a window. The famous Defenestration of Prague happened in 1618, when two imperial envoys were sent by the Habsburgs to argue with some Protestants. Their names were Slavata and Matinic, and perhaps they did not excel at conflict management because they and their secretary were thrown out of the windows of the council room of the *Hradčany* part of Prague Castle which we passed on our way to the Lobkowicz section. The envoys and secretary were not seriously hurt because they fell onto a pile of garbage or dung or both. The event brought about the Thirty Years' War. The Czechs still love to talk about it, hence the overuse of the word defenestration within the city limits of Prague.

The Lobkowicz name should be familiar to music aficionados as many from the family were generous supporters of the arts. The family's palace is now a museum and the property has an riveting history: it was confiscated by the Nazis at the beginning of World War II, and then again by the communists in 1948. William Lobkowicz, until recently an investment banker in Boston, managed to reclaim the family's property in the 1990s and had the idea to turn it into a museum. Our group was treated to lunch in one of the palace's sumptuous rooms. After lunch, we attended a short concert at which a violinist, cellist, and pianist played selections from the family's music-supporting heyday. Then we explored the museum's treasures: paintings by Canaletto, a Bruegel which is famous for being the first secular landscape painting, arms and armor, Lobkowicz family portraits, and decorative arts. The recorded tour is narrated by William Lobkowicz, the former banker and now gracious host. I bought my copy of Kafka's novel, *The Castle*, in the Lobkowicz Palace bookstore thinking I was very clever. (The novel is as complex as Prague Castle. You might describe it as "Kafkaesque.")

Audrey and I were delighted with the Lobkowicz family art treasures, but the palace's Music Room was the main event for me. Behind glass cases live manuscript scores of Beethoven's Fourth and Fifth symphonies, an early manuscript of Beethoven's Op. 18 String Quartets, a printed copy of Beethoven's Third Symphony (the "Eroica"), and a score of Handel's *Messiah* with corrections and reorchestrations by Wolfgang Amadeus Mozart. There are more scores in the collection's archives, but these are the items on display. (If there had been any more musical treasures to look at, the tour group would have lost me. I could have gaped at them all day.)

Beethoven met the seventh Prince Lobkowicz, Josef František Maximilián, when the two were in their twenties. They became friends and the Prince arranged to support Beethoven's compositional career by paying him a pension or subsidy. This income continued beyond the Prince's death until Beethoven's own in 1827. Beethoven showed his gratitude by dedicating a number of his compositions, important ones, to Prince Lobkowicz: Symphony No. 5, Symphony No. 6, the six String Quartets Op. 18, the Harp Quartet Op. 74, the Triple Concerto, and the song cycle *An die ferne Geliebte*. When you dedicate your musical compositions to someone, it is customary to send him or her a fine copy of it. That's how these precious scores came to be in the Lobkowicze's possession. Beethoven's celebrated Third Symphony, (the "Eroica,"), a quintessential specimen of this genre, was dedicated to Lobkowicz and premiered privately in the Lobkowicz's other property, Jezeří Castle, in 1804, a whole year before its public Vienna premiere.

Three years before Beethoven died, Czech composer Bedřich Smetana (1824-1884) was born. He is remembered for a multi-part symphonic work dedicated to his homeland and named *Ma Vlast* ("My Fatherland"). Each of those movements is a full symphonic poem, and the most famous of these is "Vltava," the musical depiction of the river which flows through Prague. (Germans call the same river *Die Moldau*, and the musical work is also known by both names.) This twelve-minute symphonic poem is often performed alone, without its five companions from *Ma Vlast*. I read once that Smetana believed that when a listener could tell a composer by just a few bars of his music, that composer had achieved true originality. Smetana achieved this with his stunning illustration of flowing water in "Vltava." It is extraordinary to learn that Smetana went deaf while composing *Ma Vlast*, and just as Beethoven did, continued to compose music as a deaf genius. The Vltava River, which I've heard depicted musically thousands of times live, on recordings, and stuck in my head as a mind worm, would turn out to be profoundly connected to my most enduring Prague memory.

Smetana might command Prague's musical identity, but when it comes to the written word, Prague is Kafka's city. It's almost a cliché to quote this, but I'll do it anyway: "As Gregor Samsa awoke one morning from uneasy dreams he found himself transformed in his bed into a giant insect." That's the first line from Franz Kafka's novella *Metamorphosis*, and one of the best first-lines in literature ever. This description of Samsa trying to get out of bed for the first time as a bug gives me the shivers: "He would have needed arms and hands to hoist himself up; instead he had only the numerous little legs which never stopped waving in all directions and which he could not control in the least."

Already by this point in the story, Kafka has created a deictic shift: the reader has entered a new reality where it is entirely possible for a man to wake up as an insect. The reader then learns how excruciatingly painful this is for Gregor Samsa and his family. His parents don't know how to deal with their son in this form, but his sister Grete compassionately experiments with food to find something that her brother in this new form might like to eat. She also gets her mother to help move furniture in Gregor's room to give him room to move around, but Mrs. Samsa shrieks when she makes eye contact with her son who is hiding under a quilt. That couldn't have been easy for him. (Wait—he's not real.)

Kafka did not write about music much, so it is interesting that one of Gregor's biggest concerns is how to send his violinist sister to the conservatory: "…it was a secret plan of his that she, who loved music, unlike himself, and could play movingly on the violin, should be sent next year to study at the Conservatorium, despite the great expense that would entail, which must be made up in some other way." He had made no promises, but he was worried about his earning potential as an insect and how he would pay her tuition. Kafka must have been aware of musicians in his most musical city. Could he have known a young female violinist dreaming of enrolling at a conservatory?

> I think we ought to read only the kind of books that wound and stab us... We need the books that affect us like a disaster, that grieve us deeply, like a death of someone we loved more than ourselves, like being banished into forests far from everyone, like a suicide. A book must be the axe for the frozen sea inside us.
>
> Franz Kafka, from a letter to Oskar Pollak
> (January 27, 1904)

I bristle when I recall my academic Kafka experience, but studying Kafka again caused those memories to bubble to the surface. We read Kafka's *Metamorphosis* in a college literature course focused on short stories. This was my first exposure to Kafka, and I remember being captivated by the writer's imagination. Kafka's description of Gregor Samsa's reaction to how people treated him after he woke up as a bug hit home with me. My father had a crippling stroke three years before I took that course, and I vividly remember how my nieces and nephew, then nine, eight, and five, reacted to him once he was different. They were confused and didn't know what to say or do. It was hard to watch, and I didn't know what to say to them or Dad to make it easier. I was so sure that this tough memory related to what Kafka was attempting to represent in *Metamorphosis* that I timidly raised my hand in that class and offered the memory and my analysis. Our chairs were arranged in a circle and I could see everyone's face. I was horrified to see twenty or so college-student faces staring blankly back at me. "Oh, why did I speak at all?" I asked myself. I don't usually share such personal information and feelings. The professor finally moved on to another discussion point without acknowledging my comments. I still bristle.

Thirty-two years later, I finally received vindication. I was reading about Kafka as part of my over-preparation for this Prague trip, and a scholar I was reading (Michael P. Ryan) suggested a possible inspiration for *Metamorphosis*. It was similar to my collegiate analysis, involving illness and changing interactions with people around the afflicted person. I'm not so naïve to think that that is the only possible theory, but it vindicated mine and gave me some scholarly closure. The article, "Samsa and Samsara: Suffering, Death, and Rebirth in 'The Metamorphosis'" from *The German Quarterly* (vol. 72,), goes on to describe the concept of Samsara, a centuries-old concept which includes disease, death, rebirth, and lust. I don't have to be an English professor to notice the similarity between the word *Samsara* and the *Metamorphosis* family's surname, Samsa. I wish I had that gem on the tip of my tongue in that Short Story classroom thirty-something years ago.

Last spring, a student visited my office in order to

present me with a gift. He enjoyed a course I taught, "The Evolution of the Symphony," and knowing I'm a writer, Ismael gave me a leather-covered notebook and my favorite kind of pen (including refills). It was a lovely but fleeting moment followed by an awkward conversation about travel in front of my amused office mate. We talked about places we would be visiting that summer and I mentioned how there were important rivers associated with my destinations: The Danube, the Salz, and Prague's *Vltava* which we knew from class was rendered in music by Bedřich Smetana. Grasping for something relevant to say, Ismail blurted out, "Oh, I really like rivers." I was grasping, too. My witty retort: "I really like bridges." I was just starting to realize that I notice bridges, aesthetically. Nevertheless, my comment sounded stupid and I could tell my office mate (pretending not to listen) wanted to burst out laughing. I'm pretty sure I saw tears of repressed mirth squirting out of her eyes. Now that I've metamorphosed into a professor myself, I surmise that it is not always obvious how a teacher should respond when a student says or does something unexpected, but that response can have an enduring impact on the student.

The truth is that bridges *were* on my mind. I had been working on a magazine article about a local railroad bridge over the Delaware River which I discovered was having its 100th birthday that year, the same year my father would have celebrated his own 100th birthday. I pass this bridge twice a day, going and coming from work, and its fourteen arches remind me of an ancient Roman viaduct. It's an inspiring sight lit by the morning sun or fading into twilight. Train enthusiasts know that the CSX Juice Train, a train transporting orange juice from Florida to New Jersey, passes over that bridge a few times a week. My appreciation for that bridge grew as I learned more about that bridge in particular and about bridges in general. I explored bridges as metaphors for joining things, and for building relationships between people and groups. ("Make connections; Build bridges; Add value" is my librarian-motto.) I hadn't recognized yet my habit of admiring bridges. Though considering my newly-recognized affinity for bridges it should have been obvious that the Charles Bridge would become my most enduring image of Prague, and one that connects to Kafka.

"The Bridge" is one of Kafka's later stories. A man imagines himself as a bridge spanning a creek. His coattails become rumpled, but he cannot fix them, of course, because he is now a bridge. I'm not a metaphor-detection expert, and I was unable to find any literary criticism published on this particular short, short story. (The best metaphor I can put together for this is "People are walking all over me!" Maybe that's not far from the truth.) I prefer to believe that Kafka had an affinity for bridges just as I do ("I like bridges!"), and in one of his wild daydreams as he crossed the Charles Bridge he imagined himself as the bridge.

The Charles Bridge, known as the Stone Bridge until 1870, traverses Smetana's Vltava River and connects the Old Town (*Staré Město*) to the Lesser Town (*Malá Strana*) at the foot of Castle Hill. King Charles IV set the first stone in 1357, and his larger-than-life patina-ed statue stands by the huge medieval gate on the *Staré Město* side. When it was completed in 1402, it would be the city's only bridge for 400 years. Built of Bohemian sandstone, the bridge originally had no statues, but now it is populated by life-size saints and heroes along with live street musicians and artists selling their work. The imperial Hapsburg family had those religious statues built in an attempt to re-convert formerly Protestant Hussite Czechs to Catholicism in the 17th and 18th centuries. Most of the original statues have been preserved in museums because they were showing wear from weather and pollution. We see replicas as we cross the bridge, but Kafka would have seen the real ones.

Though Kafka's writing in both his fiction and his diaries is usually gloomy and dark, he painted a pleasant picture of the Charles Bridge in his 1916 diary. After a date with a woman named Ottla, he walked home over that bridge: "Was excited by the statues of saints on the *Karlsbrücke* (The Charles Bridge). The remarkable light of the summer evening together with the nocturnal emptiness of the bridge." That little passage describing the open-ness and light is a departure from the dark, depressing, even cramped literature he usually produced.

The Madonna is on the bridge with St. Bernard, and with St. Dominick and St. Thomas Aquinas. St John of Matha and St. Felix are depicted there freeing imprisoned Christians and St. Adelbert, St. Nicholas of Tolentino, St. Vincent Ferrer, St. Procopius, and St. Francis Xavier (with his sculptor's self-portrait to his right). The most interesting of all is the bronze

Baroque statue of St. John of Nepomuk with five golden stars around his head. This fourteenth-century priest heard the queen's confessions, and when her husband, King Wenceslas IV, demanded to know her secrets, St. John of Nepomuk refused to tell. The king had him tossed off the Stone Bridge at the very location of today's statue. When the priest hit the water, five stars appeared. The unfortunate priest became a saint in 1729. This statue is the oldest on the bridge, placed there in 1683, three hundred years after the St. John of Nepomuk's death. Imagine generations of little Czech children learning their Catechism by scrutinizing these statues.

Audrey and I walked through the towering medieval *Staré Město* gate, and over the bridge to get from Old Town to Prague Castle, admiring the saints and heroes and listening to the music of a three-piece jazz ensemble. I almost forgot what we were crossing over: the Vltava! I stood between some saints to look at Smetana's river, now with more bridges across it and a few modern sightseeing boats passing beneath. Narrow canals branched off the river and wound into the red-roofed buildings on either side. I saved some images of the Vltava in my mind and in my camera to share with Ismail back at school. (He likes rivers.)

In the end, Kafka's Prague did woo me with its uniqueness: the medieval architecture, the Old Town Square, Prague Castle, Kafka's haunts, and especially the magnificent Charles Bridge. I may have been mentally exhausted from a fast-paced week of sightseeing where we woke up in a new city each day, but I left this final city with a collection of enduring images. I couldn't have predicted the brides on the square, the complexity of Prague Castle mirrored in Kafka's novel, *The Castle*, the abundant collection of Lobkowitz treasures, or the sight of the Astronomical Clock in the spring rain. In retrospect, it seems a no-brainer that the bridge would be my most exceptional Prague memory. What seemed like a goofy statement back in that conversation with Ismail doesn't seem so goofy anymore. I like bridges.

Margaret Montet

The Music of Fairies

The statue of Molly Malone with her seafood barrow has become a landmark and meeting place in Dublin.

Behind my grandfather's bright blue eyes lived an Irish storyteller's mind. He would sit in his armchair in Butler, New Jersey, with his pipe stand to his right and tell his stories to whatever grandchildren might be around. Through cherry–scented pipe aroma I would hear "Margie me gal, did I ever tell you about the time…?" When I knew him, he was a retired letter carrier with lots of time to put together his tales which seemed extemporized and customized for his audience. One in particular sticks in my mind, told as he rode shotgun in our family's Ford Granada with the bumpy plastic seat covers. My father drove through the hilly terrain of Northern New Jersey, and I sat in the backseat with my mother and Grandma. Grandpa told this tale about my father and uncles fighting off a tribe of hungry cannibals on a tropical island. My father and uncles were trying to avoid landing in the giant black stockpot the cannibals had set up over an open flame. I remember laughing so hard my sides hurt while the other adults rolled their eyes. I know the plot sounds dumb. It had to be my grandfather's storytelling that made me laugh.

I very recently realized that Grandpa's cannibal story sounds a lot like Robinson Crusoe. My father was cast in the Crusoe role, and Uncle Bill W. and Uncle Bill L. shared the duties of My Man Friday. Crusoe and Friday battled cannibals in much the same way as my father and the Uncle Bills in Grandpa's story. I can see Grandpa as a little boy reading this book, and then as a young father, reading it to my mother and her siblings. He had the air of an adventurer about him even if his days of adventure were mostly behind him when I, the youngest grandchild, finally came on the scene.

Grandpa told his stories with that wry wit and a blue–eyed sparkle as a true Irishman would. He never told (in my presence, anyway) traditional Irish tales which are so important to Irish culture. During my recent visit to that legendary lush green island, I heard many: go to a pub—hear a story. Go on a bus tour—hear a folk tale. Besides Guinness, Aran sweaters (I bought two), and Claddagh rings, folklore is probably the country's most notable export.

When I think back on my Ireland experience, it organizes itself in my mind into a musical form. Musical forms are my way of making sense of structure—I know these well from my days as a Music Theory major. My Ireland memories, now processed and organized by my musical mind, have emerged in a sonata–allegro form. (This is the form in which most Classical and Romantic symphony and sonata first–movements are composed. It's a standard template.) Dublin is the exposition, the most important 'stuff' of the piece. Ancient Tara is the development, because the ancient history builds upon what I had already learned about Ireland generally and Dublin specifically. Belfast, another Irish city, is the recapitulation because as an urban center it recalls Dublin. It is, of course, different, just as a musical recapitulation will differ from the exposition it recalls. Galway is the most Irish region culturally because of its location far west from where historic invaders and influences came ashore in the east. During this symphony of a visit, I was charmed by the indigenous folk tales and songs, and Galway seems to be the capital of folk. This is where we heard the most about fairies. There's my coda to finish off the movement.

DUBLIN: EXPOSITION

I was in Ireland with my writing program. Eighteen students and eight or so faculty called Trinity College, Dublin, "home" for two weeks while we learned to tell our own stories. I was assigned a fourth floor dorm room, so every day I climbed those hateful stairs more than once to my aerie in the sky. Forgot a notebook for a lecture? Up I'd go. Need a sweater? Up, up, up those stairs. At the end of a busy day, (they were all busy with lectures, workshops, and exploration), I would relax in my spot which was level with the Trinity College tree canopy. From the common room across the hall I had a bird's eye view of Trinity's Parliament Square including the Campanile (the bell tower where our group would collect before heading somewhere) and the Main Gate. With my window open I could hear the frequent rain hitting the leaves on the tree just outside, and the music wafting up from Grafton Street, just outside the college's wall: an electric guitar mimicking the great rock guitar solos of decades past, drunken vocalizations from outside of the pubs, and on a few occasions an electrified violin. All of this was in the air up there.

On our first morning in Dublin, fellow teller of true tales Amy W. and I began exploration by way of a travel brochure walking tour. We found our way to St. Andrew's Church and the larger–than–life–sized statue of Molly Malone with her seafood cart outside the edifice. Locals call the statue "the tart with the cart" owing to the low cut of her bodice and the centuries–old rumor that she was a prostitute in the evenings after parking her seafood cart. The statue is a meeting place in Dublin; in fact we would meet our Northern Ireland tour bus there the following weekend. Molly Malone is a fictional character, created in Irish music halls. (So, if she was a prostitute, it was because someone created her thus. We can't fault her for that.) She's a young woman who sells seafood from a wheel barrow in the streets of Dublin just as her parents did:

> In Dublin's fair city,
> Where the girls are so pretty,
> I first set my eyes on sweet Molly Malone.
> As she wheeled her wheel–barrow,
> Through streets broad and narrow,
> Crying 'Cockles and mussels, alive, alive, oh.'"

I checked YouTube for a recording of this song. There are many, by artists such as the Dubliners, the Ferrymen, and Bono, but Sinead O'Connor's version touched me most. (Did my mother sing this to me? It sounds so familiar.) She sings the song slowly, staring into the camera (at me) and yells "Cockles" and "Mussels!" as a fishmonger would, into the air above her accenting the second syllables of 'cockles' and 'mussels.' As I watched Sinead O'Connor's ethereal interpretation of "Molly Malone," I realized, from the way her performance sliced through my ribcage and directly into my heart, that my mother probably sang this to me when I was very little. I don't have a concrete memory of this but instead a vague, abstract recollection. Music is an art form which is gone as soon as it is performed except for the parts we store in an abstract memory somewhere in our complex brains. Music is storytelling, too.

Amy and I continued on our walking tour, continuing past St. Andrews Church and the Molly Malone statue, through more of the city, and finally arriving at St. Stephen's Green. This park in the center of Dublin, commissioned in 1880, was filled with birds, extra–large herring gulls, pigeons, magpies, robins, and wrens: in the air, on the pond water, and on the ground. Suddenly, from the green–leaved Sycamore branches above our heads, a plop of true Irish–green bird poo landed in my hair, on my brow, on my clean purple shirt, and on my camera. I did my best to clean up with leaves as neither of us savvy world travelers had so much as a tissue.

TARA: DEVELOPMENT

Concentric circular hills surround the Mound of the Hostages in Tara. The "hostages" here are children from various Druid families who were taken hostage to be raised in the king's house. This is important and sacred territory for Druids (ancient pagans of Ireland), Celts, and Christians, too, as Saint Patrick convinced the king here to let him preach Christianity in Ireland by the fifth century. On the day that our group toured the Hills of Tara we also popped over to Loughcrew. The skies were graying over and there were some menacing dark clouds coming our way. We climbed some steep rocky steps which led us to a grassy hill. My guidebook advises that this is a 30–minute walk. I remember our tour guide, Keith, telling us that there was a bench halfway up if we had to rest, but our reward at the top of the hill, near the cairn or burial mound, was a "better bench." My breathing became squeaky as we climbed this steep hill and the wind increased and heavy rain drenched us. I had to stop at the first bench. I sat there on the bench in my deluxe raincoat in the pouring rain to wait for my squeaky, asthmatic breathing to stop. Brianna and Chris waited with me saying they needed a rest, too, but I didn't believe them. Bob, our director, was there, asking: "You'll be okay to finish the climb after a rest, right, Margaret?" I was indeed okay after a rest, and continued up the steep, grassy mountain (actually it's a hill) to the relief of Bob, Brianna, and Chris. I skipped these details in my travel journal, but I remember them clearly now.

The elasticity of time characteristic of fairy tales had inserted itself into my own experience. When I finally arrived at the top of the hill my companions were taking turns crouching through the opening of the burial mound with tour guide Keith. This is a megalithic (meaning made of large stones) cairn dating back probably to 3300BC. It is part of a passage–tomb where multiple chambers are connected. Sliabh na Cailli is the Irish name for this site, and that translates to "mountain of the hag." According to legend, a giant hag had a load of rocks in her apron for some purpose in her garden, got tired, and dumped them here. The "better bench" Keith had promised us was the Hag's Chair, a stone formation that looks like a seat with carvings and gouges in it where the hag rested. The hag's rocks are the green gritstone boulders we see now around the landscape, and inside the mound. We saw carvings of suns inside the tomb. Keith told us that these sun carvings are placed so that rays from the summer solstice sun would hit them. As if on cue, the sun broke through the clouds that moment we were in the burial mound. We were close enough to the solstice (early July) to see the sun's rays hitting the sun carvings. That was worth the torturous climb.

BELFAST: RECAPITULATION

I will always think of Northern Ireland as wet. Amy, Kathy, Rena, Katie, Erin, Rachel, and I, writers of fiction, poetry, and nonfiction, met at the Molly Malone statue by St. Andrew's Church in the wee hours of the morning to board a bus for a day tour of Belfast and Northern Ireland. We were curious: were there still bullets flying and bombs detonating? Those troubles had tapered–off, right? The bus was luxurious. Because of the luggage compartments underneath, those bus seats ride high above the road and give the rider the sensation of rapidly cruising through the country air… until the bus hits a bump.

Our bus driver, Derrick, told us a fine story as we approached a curiosity called the Giant's Causeway near Belfast. A giant named Finn MacCool (or Fionn MacCumhaill in Irish) lived near here in County Antrim. He was a warrior–hero and tales of his adventures were later told from the point of view of his son Oisín. These were called the Fenian Cycle. In

Derrick the bus driver's story, Finn was feuding with another giant, Benandonner, from Scotland. Finn crossed the water via a causeway he had built out of stone (basalt) columns so that he could settle things with his enemy. Something happened—Finn got scared or Benandonner wasn't in—and Finn ran back to County Antrim. Mr. and Mrs. MacCool received word that Benandonner was coming for Finn and they saw this huge creature himself lumbering across Finn's causeway. Not wanting to fight such a large opponent, Finn jumped under a blanket in a cradle and his wife then convinced Benandonner that this huge baby was her youngest of fifteen. Her other enormous children were out hunting with their gargantuan father, she said. It worked: Benandonner ran back to Scotland scattering Finn MacCool's neatly constructed causeway into piles of broken rocks. We were now headed to this very Giant's Causeway! Towering cliffs, rocks of all sizes, and tall clumps of hexagonal columns of basalt rose out of the breakers and foam. I walked away with breathtaking and unique landscapes in my Nikon.

Derrick drove us on our luxury bus to Belfast. Besides the memories of violent troubles in that city that I had seen on the evening news in the past, my only connection is a sepia family photograph which I found in my mother's portion of my grandparents' things with "Belfast" etched in gold in the corner under the photographer's name. I don't know who the people are, but they were from Belfast and are related to me somehow and here I am in that same city. There's an Irish word for the kind of day we had in Belfast: doineann, which means foul weather and the stress it generates. We could have paid some extra money (British pounds here) to go on a narrated Black Taxi tour of the city, but we decided to explore on our own. Up to this point in Ireland, rain showers had been brief so we were optimistic. Days like this are called breaclá or dappled days. Sunny skies alternate with rain. Most Irish days are like this. But no, the Belfast day was an extended soaker. We were wet and cold. As I clung to the wet paper bag holding the sandwich and pastry I bought to eat when I got back to my dorm room aerie in Dublin, I listened to the other bus passengers tell the story of their fine taxi tour. They saw Belfast's famous murals and the Titanic Quarter where the famous luxury liner was built. Shoot. I missed it.

This daytrip would have pleased my storytelling grandfather as his and my grandmother's ancestors came from Protestant Northern Ireland, County Antrim to be exact, where the giant MacCool family lived.

GALWAY: CODA

Kathy and I rode the fast train from Dublin to Galway when our residency was over. The train cuts across Ireland's middle like a leprechaun's belt with the train averaging about 89 mph for the 129–mile trip. We were interested in seeing Galway, a part of Ireland less touched by Anglo influences and where one hears Irish folktales and the Irish (Gaelic) language more than other regions. While we were there, the Galway International Arts Festival was going on, and we could often hear Irish music from the streets or pubs wafting up to our hotel room. There were fiddles, Irish bagpipes, drums called bodhrans, flutes, and voices, and often soaring high above the other instruments was the tinny sopranino sound of a penny whistle which to my ear transforms this worldly music into the music of fairies. Galway also boasts a fine, central location for daytrips: Connemara, the Aran Islands, and the Cliffs of Moher were the three that Kathy and I enjoyed.

Galway has a rich Irish folk tradition owing to its geographic position far away from the influences of England, and thanks to the work of playwright and Galway native Lady Isabella Augusta Gregory (1852–1932). She promoted the arts, co–founded Dublin's Abbey Theater, and, inspired by her friends in the Gaelic League, Douglas Hyde and W.B. Yeats, volunteered to collect and edit volumes of folktales. She could speak Irish (Gaelic) as well as English and therefore had a particular interest in her native Galway region where Irish was still spoken.

Lady Gregory collected the following tale from an old man in Galway in 1902:

A man named Robin sold a cow at a Galway market and then had a wee too much Guinness afterward. Rather than go straight home, he found a spot in a barn and made a bed in a pile of straw. He woke during the night to see some men hiding stolen silver in the straw. In the morning Robin told the distressed townspeople. The good citizens retrieved the stolen goods and waited for the criminals to return for it.

Robin's landlord heard of his heroic deed and was convinced that if Robin's special powers were real, Robin should help him: "I will lock you up in a room for three days. If you can't tell me by the end of that time who stole my wife's diamond ring, I'll put you to death."

On the first evening, the butler brought Robin his supper. "There's one of them," Robin said, meaning that the first of three days was over. The butler, however, thought Robin was fingering him for the crime.

The cook brought the second day's supper: "There's two of them," Robin said, and of course we know he meant the second day was over. The cook conferred with the butler. Both were shaken, because they were, in fact, the perpetrators of the crime along with the housekeeper.

Sure enough, when the housekeeper delivered Robin's supper on the third night, he said, "There's the third," and the three jewelry thieves begged Robin to help them avoid justice.

Robin considered the situation and devised a strategy: "Go and find that big tom turkey outside and force the ring down his throat." The next day when the landlord asked Robin to reveal the identity of the thief, Robin advised the landlord to have the turkey cut open. (They were going to eat it anyway.) Sure enough, the ring was there, Robin was free, and the turkey was framed for the crime.

From Robin's town of Galway, Kathy and I took a bus tour of the Connemara region, home to thousands of black–faced Connemara sheep, peat bogs, gothic Kylemore Abbey (home to Benedictine nuns who fled Belgium during World War I), and lots of talk of fairies. Our bus driver, Martin, had a strange but pleasing way of drawing out the last syllables of sentences as he prattled on nonstop about the sheep, the Burren, the bogs, and the fairieeeeees. Fairies have no past or future and therefore have no hopes, regrets, or memorieeeeees, but they do have the ability to speed up and slow down time. Mythical invaders condemned the fairies (called Sidhe in Irish) to live underground or in trees or bushes. They frolic in merry groups around hawthorn treeeeees. At one point, Martin pulled the bus into a scenic overlook so that we could have a look at a fjord called Kilary Harbor. (A fjord is an inlet with steep sides and deep water.) More interesting to me than the fjord was a strange, permanently–windswept tree with all kinds of debris hanging from it. "That's a fairy tree," Martin said. (Away from his microphone, he didn't stretch out his syllables.) "Leave something of value and the fairies will grant your wish." He explained that fairy trees are always hawthorns, and they get their lopsided, bent–over shape from the wind. It's bad luck to chop a hawthorn tree down, so they are often found in farmers' fields with crops growing all around. I walked closer to the enchanted tree, just behind the scenic view guardrail, and realized that the colorful "junk" hanging from the tree was a collection of socks, handkerchiefs, hats, and a child's rubber Wellington. All of those people who had been here before me had sacrificed a sock or some trinket to have a chance at a wish being granted. I was traveling light and couldn't think of anything I could spare.

Does this mean I can't have my wish? (What would I wish for anyway?)

The hawthorn fairy tree beside the fjord conjured up an image of my own garden at home in New Jersey. I have a lopsided pussy willow tree, its branches next to the house pruned off so as to not disturb the house's siding. It is coincidentally precisely the shape of the fjord's windblown fairy tree. I remember planting the pussy willow myself from a stick given to me by a woman years ago at the public library. (Was that woman a fairy?) A few years ago, before I had any suspicion that my pussy willow was a fairy tree, I strung whimsical solar–powered lights, called FAIRY LIGHTS, on that pussy willow tree. Below it, I placed two tiny store–bought buildings (a fairy house made from a teapot and a wee fairy bakery), a couple of bridges over streams made of blue glass nuggets, shrubs made of magnolia seed pods, and paths made from wood slices, flower pot shards, and clamshells. Fairy gardens have been popular in gardening for the past few years, but who knew if I set one up the fairies would actually inhabit it and sculpt that pussy willow tree to match the fairy trees in Galway?

I'd explored Dublin, Northern Ireland, Tara, Connemara, and Galway and now I was to begin my descent back into my daily routine life. These places steeped in folklore seemed oddly familiar, probably because of the similarity of Grandpa's storytelling style and Mom's long–lost songs. Folktales, storytelling, and song are so much a part of Irish culture that the place seemed familiar from knowing intuitively about its folklore. The places I've described here are the ones I remember best, because they have stories associated with them, either my own or centuries–old tales. But just as with my grandfather's crazy cannibal story, the act of telling the tale or singing the song makes it extraordinary.

I learned about Ireland from its folk songs, legends, and stories. My stories are true, now, but will I be tempted to embellish them in the future? Will I be showered in green bird poo in St. Stephen's Green and live in a 15th–floor dorm room at Trinity College? Will Irish EMTs need to be called to revive me on the hill at Loughcrew shouting "CLEAR!" as the paddles touch my chest? While Irish legends and fairy tales are entertaining and give the visitor an idea of what the Irish find fun, entertaining, and important, they are not to be taken as fact. Even as a child, I didn't believe for one minute that Grandpa's cannibal story had any truth to it, but it was sure fun to hear him tell it.

I intend for my stories to be true. Nonfiction. Not exaggerated. While I seem to have inherited the feel of Irish folk stories from my maternal ancestors, I didn't inherit the gift of embellishment. But how would I know if I did? These biographical stories are true as I recollect them, but can I be sure they haven't been tainted by the stories of other travelers or my own unconscious dreams? My experiences did not actually unfold in a neat sonata–allegro form; my mind imposed that form on my memories and I liked the way it fit. Should I be skeptical about my bits of memoir since discovering this sonata–allegro sleight–of–hand? Please imagine each essay I write with a disclaimer: "The events depicted in this essay are true to the best of my recollection."

Molly Malone, the Hag of Loughcrew, Finn MacCool, and Robin of Galway could have been inspired by real people, I suppose. The stories and songs as we know them, as they were finally recorded, are fanciful. Knowing they aren't true stories doesn't make me cherish them any less. They represent Irish folk culture and provide a shared heritage for the Irish people.

Margaret Montet

Aran Encore

Kathy and I hiked this rocky path to have a look at the remains of Dún Aonghasa, a prehistoric hill fort on a cliff on the largest of the Aran Islands, Inis Mór.

As our Galway ferry arrived at the port town of Kilronan on Inishmór, we spotted the minivans lined up waiting to collect fifteen Euros from each visitor in exchange for a guided tour of this, the biggest Aran Island. Tourism is the main source of income for the natives of Inishmór, and as soon as our coach left the village of Kilronan we understood the importance of our visit. There were few structures on the island—some houses, some inns, a few small factories (one makes goat cheese), gift shops, and a small college where you can learn the Irish language (known as Gaelic to most outside Ireland). We travelers are their industry.

It was desolate and windswept, but scenically so. There was no electricity here until 1975, and even then it came from generators. We visited the stone ruins of a church, monastery, and graveyard, drove past a beach where friendly but human-shy seals live and swim in the friendly bay. As with the rest of Ireland, the real estate of Inishmór is divided by dry stone walls made of granite and quartz schist with no cement holding them together. Don't lean on them.

The Atlantic Ocean looked friendly that sunny summer day, but the tales of the Aran Islands characterize that same body of water as wild and angry. I bought a small book of Aran stories in one of the gift shops, and in every single story the focus is on survival-on the sea and in the wind. The ocean is necessary for life on the island, but the ocean also takes life away. Irish poet W.B. Yeats advised his young writer friend John Millington Synge (1871-1909) to go to the Aran Islands to collect stories as a kind of apprenticeship in Irish folklore and culture. One of Synge's stories in my little souvenir book told the story of a woman and her daughters who received a parcel containing clothing samples from a man who had drowned a distance from their home, where the woman's son had been fishing. The woman had already lost three sons and her husband to the sea. During the excruciating drama surrounding the opening of the parcel (the clothes did indeed belong to that matriarch's son), her other son drowned close to home and was carried to the house to be laid out on the dining room table. The ocean had taken the woman's last two sons within a week. Synge fashioned a play from this tale in 1904.

Once I visited a tea shop back home in Cape May after a big storm. I asked the proprietress about her experience riding out the storm in town, and she called the Atlantic "the Angry Ocean." The comment took me by surprise because that is the same friendly, familiar ocean I began swimming in when I was a toddler. I never considered that it had an angry mood, but the other side of this same ocean took that woman's five sons and husband in the J.M. Synge play.

The Man of Aran is a 1934 black and white film (the Irish say "filum") about a small family on the Aran Islands and the drama they encounter. The woman collects red kelp or seaweed from the ocean and carries it in a basket on her back up the rocky coastline to their small property. The seaweed would be used as fertilizer for their small potato crop or be burned for heat. The man goes out in his Curragh, the typical wood-framed boat covered with calf hide and then covered with tar.

We get to see him mending a tear in the boat skin in the film. Back when we were cruising through Connemara, bus driver Martin pointed out a Curragh to us in the Galway Bay to our left. With the rather large oars used to propel the boat, (three or four on either side), the boat looked like a bug. (I read that even the islanders think these boats look like bugs when the men carry them over their heads to the water. The boat is the bug's body and the men's legs are the bug's legs.) Out in Galway Bay and the Atlantic Ocean, the fishermen will fish mainly for mackerel with nets or bream with lines. Further back in Aran history, fishermen hunted for basking sharks because they supplied oil for lamps. The filum shows this even though it is an anachronism— shark hunting ended decades before the time of the movie and its characters. Director Robert Flaherty was accused of overdramatizing the events in the film, but he did portray clearly the changing personalities of the ocean. The movie resonated with me--it's a riveting, uniquely-Irish story.

My travel buddy, Kathy, and I agreed that the most memorable point on this island is Dùn Aonghusa (the name sounds like 'done angus'), the ancient fort built along the Atlantic cliffs somewhere around 400 B.C. (Scientists don't agree on the date.) Our minibus dropped us off a few steps from its visitors' center from which we launched on a long hike up a rocky hill to see the fort. At one point I stopped, turned around, and shot a photo that illustrates the magnitude of this arduous climb for the people back home. (I am not exaggerating about these climbs!) I was about halfway at this point, and the climb would soon get steeper and rockier. Finally we got to the fort, three concentric semicircular rock walls with the ruins of a stone structure in the middle. The half-circles open up on the 330-foot-high cliffs and then the Atlantic Ocean below. You caught that, right? The cliffs are more than an American football field high.

The Fir Bolg people built this fort along with others in Ireland. This tribe seemed to always be at war with other tribes and were pushed around Ireland, then Scotland, and then to Inishmór. The last of the tribe, King Aengus sat at Dùn Aonghusa to lament the death of his only son Conall who had been killed by the sword of the legendary Cúchulainn. The sword was one of those legendary ones which had a name: *Gae Bulga*. (I'll point out here that we've entered the realm of "truthiness." I'm not sure where history ends and legend begins because these tales have been told as history for centuries, probably modified with each telling. They are not reliable sources for historical facts. Oral tradition has taken over and proper citations have been lost. My professional librarian opinion is to treat storytelling of any kind as entertainment, but it is still fascinating.) This Cúchulainn character, when he was a boy, accidentally killed his king's guard dog with a hurley (the stick used to this day in the game of hurling) and felt so bad that he took over the dog's job of guarding the king. Cúchulainn grew up to be a brave warrior, and it was he who killed King Aengus's son Conall who would have been on his way to be king of the dwindling Fir Bolg people.

Conall's father, the king, sat on the very rocks on which Kathy and I climbed on to think his way through his son's death. His son and their legacy were gone. Who would save his people? After some time, he took up his helmet and shield and went off to die fighting the enemies of his people.

I didn't have this story straight in my mind while we were climbing around on those rocks. Dùn Aonghusa was impressive enough with only a vague notion of the legends. When our time there was up, we left Dùn Aonghusa, and we walked down the long, rocky path. This is the first time in Ireland that I remember descending. I always seemed to be walking up hills, climbing up cliff paths, and crawling up stairs. The old quip of a round-trip being "uphill both ways" seemed to be the theme of my Irish excursions.

Inishmór's remoteness reminds me of my hometown, Cape May. While most of Cape May's tourists descend upon that city by car, bus, and by ferry in June and leave by Labor Day, most of Inishmór's tourists show up as we did on the ferry for just the day. If the water is too choppy, the ferries won't run. While the tourists are in either place, there's liveliness and commerce. When the visitors go away, there is quiet seclusion, and harsher weather is likely. I hated this remoteness as a kid even though I was only subjected to it for a week or a weekend at a time, although I admit it was glorious when my cousins were there. My parents were busy with home maintenance chores and visiting their friends from when they lived there year 'round. I read books, sprawled-out on the bed in front of a box fan in the bedroom with two windows or on the porch couch with the incredible sea breezes. Now as an adult I long to go to Cape May to lose myself in a book or writing project, but now I'm the one doing home maintenance projects.

The remoteness of Inishmór appeals to me in much the same way. I imagine the quiet, delectable solitude of summertime in Inishmór: visitors during the day, and quiet reading, writing in the evening. Perhaps there would be good conversation, too, and book discussions! Always, I would be watching the many moods of Galway Bay and the Atlantic Ocean.

My Precious Cape May Point

A great egret poses in the marshy Cape May Point State Park. The Cape May Lighthouse is barely visible in the fog behind the trees.

Not much happens in Cape May Point unless you know where to watch. From the breezy top of the lighthouse to the wooded nature trails to the desert landscape around the World War II Lookout Tower, life happens. Birds, bees, dolphins, and people put on a show every day for the attentive observer. Gulls steal sandwiches. I struggle to identify the birds who have been part of this environment for centuries.

My parents landed in Cape May in the late 1940s because my dad was stationed at the U.S. Coast Guard base there. By the time I came along, this former Louisiana Bayou, and then Chicago, boy had learned about the sea life and the flora at the Delaware Bay Beach near our house. He taught me about oysters, horseshoe crabs, and razor clams on our many walks. He taught me how to fly fish, a skill I've never used in adult life, and he tried to teach me about shorebirds. I regret most profoundly my lack of interest in learning about birds from him then because I struggle with bird identification now. I wish I had learned about birds from Dad. Through self-study, I can now distinguish a Herring Gull from a Laughing Gull, and I can pick out an American Oystercatcher because of its long orange beak. I can point out terns in Cape May Point State Park only because I know where they perch on that old wooden structure with the "No Trespassing" signs on it. The only bird I remember from Dad is the distinctive white Great Egret, because he told me he remembered them from his childhood in Louisiana.

While thinking about what to tell you about Cape May Point, I made a point to sit on the beach at Cape May Point State Park. It's an unguarded beach where swimming is not allowed, but it is my favorite spot for thinking and writing. This is where that Laughing Gull with the black head landed on my head and stole the pulled pork sandwich out of my hand and then had the audacity to eat it in front of me. There's the sand-colored lighthouse behind my spot, the moss-covered ruins of a World War II bunker to my left, and, if I'm lucky, a pod of dolphins swimming in front of me. Boat and Sea-Doo motors compete with the sound of the crashing waves. The Park Ranger in his noisy John Deere 4x4 patrols with his eye out for scofflaws—mostly beachgoers going into the water past their knees. (No swimming!) His 4x4 adds an aroma of gasoline to the scene. Small airplanes fly overhead with block-lettered advertisements trailing behind, and no matter what book is open on my lap, I have to look up to read those messages. Best of all is the steady sea breeze on a hot day. Owing to my position at the southern end of the peninsula of New Jersey, I enjoy the benefits of sea breezes from the east, south, and west. They flip the pages of my book but I don't care. This is my bliss.

I don't feel like I've been to Cape May Point unless I've been to the lighthouse. Last year, there was a full moon on what would have been my father's 100th birthday, and Cape May Mid-Atlantic Center for the Arts and Humanities ("MAC"), the organization which takes care of the lighthouse, hosted a Full-Moon Climb. I've been to these before, but last year's was particularly popular making it necessary for me to wait in line with the heat, humidity, and mosquitos. Eventually, I had my chance to climb the 199 wrought-iron steps to the top where there are fewer mosquitoes, refreshing breezes, and magnificent views.

From the top of the lighthouse at night the sky seems to melt into the Atlantic Ocean to the south and east, and the Delaware Bay to the west. It's difficult to spot where the sky ends and the water begins. Twinkling lights from ships at sea dot the water like those tiny colorful balls on a nonpareil candy. Stars in the sky do likewise. Near where the horizon should be, I can't tell which is which. The moon's reflection on the water looks like a sparkling path to the horizon. There's an exotic Swedish word for this, mångata. On this evening the moon is positioned just east creating a striking *mångata*. In the distance, I can see the illuminated amusement rides and neon signs of honkytonk Wildwood, our neighbor to the northeast where the young go to find good times and good pizza. Closer to the lighthouse, I see the warm yellow window-glow of the quiet homes in Cape May Point, North Cape May (to the north where my family house is), and Cape May City (to the east). It's breezy up there, and remarkably cool after a hot summer day.

My dad would have liked the Full-Moon Lighthouse Climb. He didn't go in for touristy things, but this combines a natural event, the full moon, with a Cape May landmark, the lighthouse. For most of the time he lived in North Cape May full-time (the 1950s and 1960s), the light was less of a tourist attraction and more of a navigational aid for sailors like him. He never got to climb it: the lighthouse was restored and opened to the public in the 1980s but this was after his debilitating stroke. For me, the climb is a little piece of

Cape May authenticity and he would have approved.

After our moonlit lighthouse descent, more calf-painful than the ascent, Rich the Lighthouse Keeper told our group to look up. There was the rotating beam of light shooting out from the gigantic lens at the top of the tower. It appeared light blue against the dark blue night sky from the ground, but I know the sailors out there see a white beam. (I know because I've seen it from the ferry.) It's extraordinary to see the blue beam from this perspective, and so far I have not been able to capture the magical sight with my camera.

Rich the Lighthouse Keeper is not really a lighthouse keeper (the light is automated and tended by the U.S. Coast Guard), but he plays one for tourists. Besides shepherding people up and down the tower and answering hundreds of questions, he gives talks about the lighthouse on summer Sunday mornings. Rich works with Cape May's Mid-Atlantic Center for the Arts and Humanities ("MAC") and as part of that job he also ushers visitors at the nearby World War II Observation Tower and gives talks about the music of World War II. He's not a birder. I sat down with him one day to find out what it was like to be a kid in Cape May Point back in the 1950s and 1960s. During his childhood, he was there every summer with a whole lot of cousins getting into mischief and cooking hotdogs on beach bonfires. "We'd run around barefoot all summer," he told me, "and by August we wouldn't even notice when we stepped on the yellow-flowered wild cactus native to Cape May Point." The Cape May Point Rich remembers from his childhood was a scruffier, less-developed place, but he wouldn't want to live anywhere else.

The lighthouse wasn't a tourist destination during Rich's childhood. In fact, it was off-limits to civilians. Kids are kids though, so he and his cousins used to go exploring on the lighthouse grounds as much as possible. Imagine the thrill for them when the lighthouse opened for visitors in the 1980s and Rich eventually became one of our esteemed "lighthouse keepers."

On one beach day last year, I noticed the dolphins as I submerged my feet in the cool water. They were more active than usual, about fifty yards away from me. One small dolphin jumped and dove athletically enough to show anyone interested his tail flukes. Usually we beach observers just see their curved backs and dorsal fins above the water as they swim by. I was admiring Flipper's spirit when my attention was shifted to a greyish-white bird in the water who seemed to be having difficulty. One wing was extended awkwardly and small waves were washing over her head. A couple of girls walking the strand stopped to try to figure out what might be wrong. A fisherman came running over with a knife, suspecting his daughter's fishing line had tagged the bird's wing. He cut some lines leading to the bird but it still seemed to be in trouble. A small crowd had formed around me to watch the proceedings, and from this crowd my hero emerged. That guy with the white shirt and black shorts walked behind the bird, and in spite of the bird's squawking protests, he calmly grabbed both wings so that the fisherman with the knife could cut more fishing line off the bird. She was finally set down onto the shallow water, and after a few false starts, flew away, thus relieving the acute helpless anxiety I felt during the ordeal. I was so focused on the bird's terrified face that I failed to note her identifying characteristics so that I could consult my bird books later. In retrospect, I remember her coloring, her pointy wings, her long yellow beak, and her approximate wingspan when the guy in the white shirt bravely held her wings wide open. (He kind of reminded me of Dad. Dad would have done that.)

My official amateur opinion is that this bird was a Northern Gannet, not terribly unusual around here, but up to now, not a bird I recognize. According to my Kaufman bird guide, it probably wasn't. According to my Peterson's bird guide, it probably was. I'm still trying to figure out where the fishing line came from. It wasn't the little girl's because as all this was happening, she hooked a tiny sand shark. No one noticed that event besides her father and me.

Before my parents bought our house nearby, and before young Rich was running around "The Point" with cousins, this region was active in World War II homeland security. My parents never talked about this, so I started my research from scratch. There were German submarines (U-boats!) in the ocean just beyond my beach. They torpedoed a U.S. ship in the beginning of the war. (No one but history buffs talked about this for years.) There was a military base at Cape May then and another at Cape Henlopen, Delaware, across the bay to guard the Delaware Bay and River. Ports to the north shipped war supplies, so the river had to be secured. The sites on this tour are remnants from those tense days and two are especially important to Cape May Point.

That enormous concrete structure on the beach at Cape May Point was a bunker during the 1940s, working in tandem with a couple of others at Cape Henlopen in Delaware. Today this structure sits on the sand with moss growing on it and "Keep Out" signs posted all around. The salt air has not been kind to the concrete through the decades, and it has been deemed too far gone to restore. Forster's Terns seem to like the area around the bunker—whole flocks of them stand around it on hot summer beach days. (They might be Common Terns, but I'd have to spend more time with them to really know.) It took me a while to notice the terns since they have the same coloring as herring gulls and mingle with them.

The World War II Lookout Tower (technically in Lower Township but geographically closer to the center of Cape May Point) was restored in 2009. I was thrilled then to finally learn what this tall, austere concrete cylinder was and to climb the stairs to the top. We visitors get to climb convenient stairs today, but World War II military personnel had to use ladders. This cylinder, about three stories tall, stood next to the road to Sunset Beach for all of my life and a couple of decades before. It used to be called the Fire Control Tower, and briefly during the war soldiers would watch from here for enemy vessels in the ocean and bay. Through triangulation, personnel in another tower in Cape May City and soldiers here would be able to get a fix on the enemy and inform shooters in the concrete beach bunker. Their communication technology was primitive (telephone wires, for example), so this strategy was soon abandoned.

The tower stands near an abandoned magnesite plant. My mother told me that this plant was built in World War II to manufacture magnesite from salt water and limestone. (Bricks of magnesite were needed to line factory furnaces and were especially precious during the war.) The factory closed in 1983, and has since been demolished. What remains is a curious desert-like area resulting from the magnesite plant's noxious fumes. These killed vegetation all around including on the grounds of the Lookout Tower. Adding to the tower's mystique, it seems to be standing in a New Jersey desert with yellow-flowered wild Cape May Point cacti scattered about. Due to the lack of vegetation here, it is not a birding hotspot, but there are few trees and a clear view of the sky. I was standing near the tower last year when there was some commotion about something flying overhead. I asked the two otherwise taciturn guys standing near me about the creature causing the stir. "Oh, that was an immature bald eagle. There's a nest near here." Immature bald eagles are brown and don't have the distinctive white head. I wouldn't have identified this eagle unless he was wearing a sign.

Cape May Point is the accomplished birder's utopia. Besides its distinction as America's Oldest Seashore Resort, Cape May is home to some of the best birding in the world. If I could live anywhere, I'd choose this 0.3 square-mile seaside borough at the southern tip of New Jersey with the circular park in the middle, its own lighthouse, World War II artifacts, and the Atlantic Ocean and Delaware Bay for neighbors. Cape

May Point is surrounded on three sides by water, and naturally, the water helps draw me and all those yet-to-be-identified birds to this place. There's the ocean, there's the bay, there's the bird hangout Bunker Pond in Cape May Point State Park, and there in the middle of town is charming Lake Lily, a spring-fed lake with its own island. Lily is a popular birding spot and it is catnip for photographers, too. You would think that with an ocean and bay to look at, a small lake would be an afterthought, but no, it is just too darn charming.

Personally, I am not a skilled birder, but I put forth an effort. My method of birding looks like this: I take photographs of interesting birds, enlarge them on my laptop, and then compare my photos with pictures in books. It's a slow process and means that when I pack my car for a weekend at the shore, I nerdishly include a bag of bird identification books: Sibley's, Peterson's, Kaufman's, and Dunne's, at least. My complete birding reference collection is no less than ten volumes, and sometimes I consult all of them trying to make an ID. Except for a few distinct varieties, I don't make identifications in the field. I'm just not good at this. I've decided the time has come to be proactive about this birding thing, so I'll be studying those birding books, hiking the nature trails, and attending workshops and guided walks particularly in Cape May Point. I have to learn to recognize the birds.

Hanging around birders is fascinating. One sultry summer day, I was standing on the Cape May Point State Park's Hawk Watching Platform near the lighthouse shooting some landscapes featuring the bird-filled Bunker Pond. The man standing next to me was looking through his tripod Swarovski viewing scope.

"Did you see the Glossy Ibis through your camera?"

"Uh, no."

"Look through my scope: over there to the left, on that little island next to the Great Egret."

Thanks to Dad, Great Egrets are a variety I can identify, so I had no difficulty locating the dark Glossy Ibis with the rosy sheen through the man's advanced optics. "I drove all the way from North Carolina to see that," he said. I wonder if he has a bag of bird identification books in the trunk of his car.

Non-birders visiting Cape May Point State Park can also enjoy the place. I recommend a walk through the marsh mallows. Also called rose mallows, they are a type of wild hibiscus that thrives in the marsh. The park is filled with these soft-colored flowers, and its nature trails take hikers through fields of them. They are as tall as me, and feature white or pink petals with dark pink middles and yellow stamens. Marshmallows, the candy, were originally made from the gooey nectar of these flowers.

The flowers don't have much of a scent but they are a visual delight. The boardwalk or wooden trail through the biggest flowery field is a joy to walk through, snapping photos of the blooms from far away (a field of thousands) or super close-up. My photographs of these fields of flowers resemble Impressionist paintings. Butterflies and dragonflies flourish here. July and August are the best months to visit the rose mallows and be surrounded by their wild pastel beauty.

See those bees buzzing around my ankles? Don't be alarmed. They are harmless. They buzz over to the rose mallow flowers to extract the nectar and then burrow into holes in the packed-sand path. They won't bite, but it is unnerving to have bees buzzing around your legs as you walk. By the way, they take their name from the flower: rose mallow bees. I learned what I know about these bees from the park's faded informational signs.

Whenever I mention to people that I am originally from Cape May, I can count on getting this question: "Oh, the Sunken Ship! Is that still there?" It is. The S.S. Atlantus was one of four experimental World War I concrete ships. As you might predict, concrete did not make for an effective ship material, and the Atlantus was retired and towed to Cape May to be used for a ferry dock. It broke loose during preparations and ran aground off Sunset Beach in 1926. It was left there off Sunset Beach on the bay side of Cape May Point and became an unexpected tourist attraction. Today it no longer looks like a ship but rather concrete slabs with rusty rebar sticking out. That's at low tide. At high tide you can barely see any of it anymore.

For decades now, the sunken ship has directed pebbles to the beach at the end of their journey down the Delaware River and Bay from the Delaware Water Gap. The pebbles' rough edges are smoothed as they tumble on their trip down the river, past towns like Easton, New Hope, Trenton, Bristol, Salem, Sea Breeze, East Point, and finally Cape May. Some of these tumbling pebbles are made of quartz. When they wash up on the beach, eagle-eyed beachcombers will snatch them up and have them polished and cut--with facets--as a diamond would be. Known as Cape May Diamonds, they make impressive, inexpensive, sparkling-clear jewelry. People mistake mine for real diamonds all the time, but no, the set cost me less than fifty bucks.

I don't have any bird stories from Sunset Beach, but while walking along the bay with my Shetland Sheepdog, Gladys, about a mile further north, I saw an enormous brown bird perched on the sand ahead of us. I had never seen such a large bird, and I was beginning to be concerned for my chubby little Sheltie. The bird took flight and I took many photos of it as it flew over us like a runaway kite. When we got to the place where it was perched, I saw the large footprint in the sand, almost as big as my own. Later I blew up the photos I took of the big brown bird. Sure it could have been a very large hawk, or a turkey vulture, but from the shape of the beak, and the markings of the wings I'm pretty sure what we saw was another immature bald eagle. (Turkey vultures have a distinctive ugly red head which this bird did not have.) That was exhilarating.

A few local history books share space in my bag with the birding books. I don't just carry them around; I sometimes consult them. How many of those birders and photographers are aware that during the War of 1812, British sailors came ashore here to fill up their water jugs with Lake Lily water? Local residents outsmarted the British by digging a trench to connect Lake Lily with the Delaware Bay. This made the water salty and undrinkable for both the British and the

American patriots, but it was worth the price. After the British left the area, the Americans filled in the trench and eventually Lake Lily's fresh water was restored.

This summer, remembering my vow to take definitive steps to learn how to bird, I signed up for a workshop at the Cape May Bird Observatory (CMBO), in the woods across the street from Lake Lily. The workshop would be led by esteemed birder and writer, Pete Dunne. Staring at the cover of his book that morning, I thought, "I should read some of this before the workshop so it's not all brand-new." I was reminded of a favorite music professor who chided us thus: "You don't soak up any knowledge by owning fabulous books. You have to read them."

I sat with Pete Dunne's book for an hour or so and immediately learned a few things:

1. In order to make any progress with birding, I would have to acquire birding binoculars.
2. I was wearing the exact wrong colors for birding: the white shorts and a bright orange T-shirt I was wearing would not only alert birds to my presence, but probably make them nervous, too. The last thing I wanted to encounter was a nervous bird.
3. The robin is the first bird up in the morning.

Re-clad in tan, I set out for the CMBO. I have to admit I was nervous about meeting this respected expert.

I was the first to arrive (a symptom of nerd travel) and I met Pete. We talked about binoculars and his books. Once everyone else showed up, he began the workshop with this advice, also in the book: "Buy the best binoculars you can afford, and buy them as soon as you can." He covered everything I wanted to know: the best places to bird in Cape May Point, birding books (his own and others) to add to my birding reference collection, and recordings of bird song. This last is of particular interest because I often hear birdsong outside when I am inside, without a visual. Pete was very patient with our binocular questions and let us try a few of his favorite entry-level "bins." I took his advice and I now have optics: I bought a pair made by Zeiss. We learned an insider trick from Pete: if the lenses or eyepieces get grungy from birding in the salt air and you are without proper lens cleaning supplies, lick the glass! It sounds disgusting, but that tip might come in handy one day.

Our workshop group of ten went outside in the stifling July heat for a brief sample of bird finding. In that fifteen minutes we saw and/or heard a robin, a cardinal, a blue jay, a purple martin, a mourning dove, and a chimney swift. Pete Dunne was expert at identifying the birds' songs, so we didn't have to see them to identify them. I don't know if I will remember the songs of the blue jay, cardinal, and robin, but they were clearly identified that afternoon. I bought a compact disc collection of birdsong to get my ears involved in the bird identification effort.

I excavated Mom and Dad's old photo albums to look for a photograph he might have taken of birds. He brought his camera with him when he was stationed on the western Pacific islands of Palau, Guam, and Saipan, and brought his film home to Cape May to develop in the basement. I thought this collection would be the best bet for bird pictures. I found a crab close-up, a big lizard portrait, lots of palm trees, one-story concrete barracks from many angles, and one of Dad in his sailor suit holding his accordion-bellows camera.

There were no pictures of birds to wrap up my story. It occurred to me, though, that Dad must have learned a lot about the flora and fauna of these tropical islands during the 1940s and 1950s and he brought that knowledge back to Cape May. Cape May is not tropical, but its climate is a lot milder than Brooklyn's and Chicago's. All of this happened during an anxious time that was of great consequence to him, well before I was born. By the time I knew him, he was just Dad, who really liked birds.

Parting Thoughts from Margaret

While I never intended to write a memoir, I realized that we learn so much through travel that it's almost impossible to not include elements of memoir when describing a place. We need those thoughts to make sense of the unfamiliar, whether it's a quick anecdote about my mother greeting the shoe store proprietor in my hometown or my father's steadfast Roman Catholic faith. It could be the humor of the Strauss waltzes playing in a never-ending loop in the hotel breakfast room until they take on a nightmarish hue, or the surprising serenity of a medieval cathedral in Barcelona. These mental impressions, synthesized with the visual scenes and interactions with people, form my portrayals of place in *Nerd Traveler*.

Like many others in the Baby Boomer generation, my parents were gone, the marriage didn't work out, and I could go wherever I wanted and with anyone I chose! I could travel by myself if I wanted to because, ladies, that's okay now! There are horizons to stretch and places to see.

I kept travel journals and site notes, and I crafted stories about travel. Gradually, my impressions of places inspired contemplation and comprehension of what was going on inside me. I thought about the lessons my parents taught me, the facets of my identity with which I longed to reconnect, and the unfamiliar cultures I longed to understand.

I'll call it a collection of travel essays, but we all understand that it's also a memoir. Either way, as travel essays or as a memoir, I think *Nerd Traveler* will find its audience with members of the Baby Boomer generation, women travelers, solo travelers, and non-adventurous experiential travelers.

In other words, I hope mindful travelers will see aspects of themselves in *Nerd Traveler*.

**MARGARET'S FAVORITE BOOKS
ON TRAVEL AND WRITING,**
AND SOME OTHER TREASURES

Berger, John. *Ways of Seeing.* Penguin, 1977.

Bryson, Bill, and Jason Wilson, editors. *Best American Travel Essays 2016.* Mariner, 2016.
The essays in this annual collection are consistently great travel writing, and this is my favorite year.

De Botton, Alain. *The Art of Travel.* Vintage, 2004.

Calvino, Italo. Six Memos for the Next Millennium. Mariner, 2016.

Dillard, Annie. *Pilgrim at Tinker Creek.* Harper & Row, 1974.
---. *The Writing Life.* HarperPerennial, 1989.
Annie Dillard is one of my top-tier writers and top influencers. Anything I write while I'm reading her comes out sounding like a weak imitation. She gets in my head.

Iyer, Pico. *The Lady and the Monk.* Vintage, 1992.
---. "Why We Travel." Salon, 18 Mar 2000, www.salon.com/2000/3/18/why/. Accessed 23 June 2021.
Pico Iyer is one of my favorite writers. Check out his TED Talks as well.

Karr, Mary. *The Art of Memoir*. HarperCollins, 2015.

Macfarlane, Robert. *Landmarks*. Penguin, 2015.
---. *The Old Ways*. Penguin, 2012.

Malcolm, Janet. *Forty-one False Starts: Essays on Artists and Writers*. Farrar, Straus and Giroux, 2014.
Brilliant, especially the eponymous essay.

Richardson, Robert D. *First We Read, Then We Write: Emerson on the Creative Process*. University of Iowa Press, 2009.

Steinbeck, John. *Travels with Charley*. Penguin, 1980.

Steves, Rick. *Travel as a Political Act*. Rick Steves, 2018.

Acknowledgements

I didn't create these essays by myself. An all-star constellation of friends, family, teachers, readers, and supporters helped me in myriad ways. This is my chance to thank them, publicly and permanently, as if that could ever be enough. Some of these names belong in more than one category, and all of the people behind the names deserve my eternal, sincere thanks.

First, my parents and sister in heaven, also known as my guardian angels, have always been superlatively supportive. On earth, two stand-out friends-who-are-also-cousins, Janet Darcy and Margaret DesJardins, have been cheering for *Nerd Traveler* and me for a long time. I don't share DNA with the following lovely people, but they have been cheerleaders, too, some since *Nerd Traveler* was just a twinkle in my eye: Jenn Diamond-Amorello, Elizabeth Luciano, Charlie Groth, Dr. Christine Castillo, Bill Hemmig, Brian Johnstone, Monica Kuna, and Joe Shakely. Sincere thanks to all of you for listening to my incessant chatter about this project…incessantly. Samantha and Adam at Read Furiously, you two have been fantastic!

Jason Wilson and Jake Lamar, my two inspiring, stellar mentors from the Pan European MFA program at Cedar Crest College helped me shape these essays and remove the dumb stuff. Jason's voice telling me that every essay needs a payoff for the reader haunts me still, and my essays are better for it! Thoughtful advice and comments also came from these readers: Keija Parssinen, Diana Spechler, Jessica Klimesh, Kathy Kehrli, David Roth, Amy Lee Lillard, Amy Webber, Fred Peters, and my late sister Audrey who read and commented on the manuscript before she left us.

Seeing a place through another traveler's eyes is invaluable for a travel writer. *Nerd Traveler's* perspectives were enhanced by my travel companions, Jessica Klimesh, Jeanne Tinney, Kathy Kehrli, Kerri Tollinger, Alison Wellford, all the students and faculty from the Cedar Crest residencies, and my late sister Audrey who turned me on to travel tours by bus and longship. Solo travel has its perks, but exploring with a companion is invaluable. Here's a shout-out, too, to the anonymous travelers on trains and buses who have no idea they are in this book. What would I do without you?

Reading prose aloud helps a writer with flow and rhythm. Fred Peters listened from the grey recliner as I read multiple drafts of each essay these past few years from the red couch. Somehow, he never tired of this and he supplied some great feedback, too. Thank you, Fred, for listening and never getting tired of pizza or meatball sandwiches for dinner after a long day of writing! I couldn't have done it without you.

Photo credit: *Wendy Tumminello*

Margaret Montet is a college librarian and professor who writes and speaks about music, blending in elements of memoir, travel, art, and literature. She earned her MFA in Creative Writing from the Pan-European Program at Cedar Crest College, and a Master's in Music Theory from Temple University. In-between, she earned a Master of Library Science degree from Rutgers University. Margaret teaches Effective Speaking to college students and presents multimedia talks to community audiences around the southeastern Pennsylvania and central New Jersey region. Her creative nonfiction has been published in *The Bangalore Review, Clever Magazine, Dragon Poet Review, Pink Pangea, Flying South*, and other fine periodicals and anthologies. Her collection of travel essays, *Nerd Traveler*, was published July 2021 by Read Furiously.

Visit her at www.margaretmontet.com.

A Note to our Furious Readers

From all of us at Read Furiously, we hope you enjoyed our latest title, *Nerd Traveler*.

There are countless narratives in this world and we would like to share as many of them as possible with our Furious Readers.

It is with this in mind that we pledge to donate a portion of these book sales to causes that are special to Read Furiously and the creators involved in *Nerd Traveler*. These causes are chosen with the intent to better the lives of others who are struggling to tell their own stories.

Reading is more than a passive activity – it is the opportunity to play an active role within our world. At Read Furiously, its editors and its creators wish to add an active voice to the world we all share because we believe any growth within the company is aimless if we can't also nurture positive change in our local and global communities. The causes we support are culturally and socially conscious to encourage a sense of civic responsibility associated with the act of reading. Each cause has been researched thoroughly, discussed openly, and voted upon carefully by our team of Read Furiously editors.

To find out more about who, what, why, and where Read Furiously lends its support, please visit our website at readfuriously.com/charity

Happy reading and giving, Furious Readers!

Read Often, Read Well, Read Furiously!

Look for these other great titles from

Read Often. Read Well.

CPSIA information can be obtained
at www.ICGtesting.com
Printed in the USA
LVHW041446180721
693014LV00010B/1777